Items should be returned to the library from which they were borrowed on or before the date stamped above, unless a renewal has been granted.   LM6.108.5

Wiltshire
COUNTY COUNCIL

BYTHESEA
ROAD

EDUCATION & LIBRARIES

TROWBRIDGE

100%
recycled paper.

D1639735

FALCONRY
On a Wing and a Prayer

Falconry
On a Wing and a Prayer

Nick Hammond

The Crowood Press

First published in 2000 by
The Crowood Press Ltd
Ramsbury, Marlborough
Wiltshire SN8 2HR

British Library Cataloguing-in-Publication Data

A catalogue record for this book is available from the British Library.

ISBN 1 86126 323 6

To Mum and Dad; you sparked the torch that lights my love of the countryside. It burns brighter still.

Designed and edited by Focus Publishing, Sevenoaks, Kent

Printed and bound by T.J. International, Padstow, Cornwall

Frontispiece: The classic, noble stature of the falcon.

CONTENTS

ACKNOWLEDGEMENTS

It would be improper of me not to mention first and foremost Phil Gooden, who has inspired me (and hundreds more across the country) to take up this glorious sport. For allowing me to photo your beautiful birds, for the help, advice, golden days of hawking and endless hours of chats over tea – thanks mate.

Thanks must also go to Tor Hills for her invaluable efforts with the line drawings and silhouettes; as always, Tor, I end up relying on you – and you always come up trumps. The biggest thanks photography-wise must go to Brian Badger, for many of his excellent pictures are reproduced within. Thanks, Brian, your help was invaluable. Thanks also to Andy Keech for some of the photos in this book, and for his processing expertise, and to Ian 'Wally' Wassell, who gave up his time to help me with some of the more tricky shots. Cheers, Wal.

Many thanks to Steve Larner, who conjured up the name of the book and was generally amusing about its contents during its completion; thanks to Dave Ashton and, of course, Al for looking after me, and thanks to Dave's wife Marion for storing day-old cockerels in her freezer!

Thanks to Ian Pearson at Falconry Originals for advice, chats and top-quality equipment. Thanks to Marcus Amy for tirelessly supplying man, van, tools and humour (not always in that order), and thanks to Geoff and Rosita Hills for keeping their eyes peeled for falconry books in their ceaseless tour of the world's second-hand bookshops.

Thanks are also due to Editor Julie McRobbie for her cheerful encouragement, and to those at The Crowood Press for giving me this opportunity.

Finally, thanks to all who know me and have supported this project; any mistakes herein are, of course, entirely my own.

PREFACE

IS FALCONRY FOR ME?

Perhaps you have recently seen a bird-of-prey demonstration at a village fête or county show, or been to one of several bird-of-prey centres around the country, and this has piqued your curiosity. Or perhaps you have simply always had an interest in raptors and want to find out more about them. Whatever your reason, over the course of this book I hope to enlighten you about this most fascinating and ancient of sports.

The book is entitled *On a Wing and a Prayer,* not to belittle the actions and training of the falconer; the sport is not just a 'hit and hope' affair. But even the most ardent falconer could not argue with the fact that once the bird is free of human encumbrances, she is able to fly wherever she likes. For this reason alone she always carries a little prayer with her as she goes.

A word of warning: the definition of falconry is simple – the taking of wild quarry in its natural habitat by a trained bird of prey. This is the heart of our sport, and must remain so if the art is to continue unmolested. You cannot call yourself a falconer until you have trained a bird and it has taken live quarry. This is the unwritten rule.

If you fancy keeping a bird of prey simply to sit on its perch, or to show it off to friends, or merely to fly it to the fist occasionally, I suggest you find yourself a friendly local falconer, or make sure your trips to bird-of-prey centres are regular enough to satisfy your curiosity. Keeping a bird of prey for any of the reasons listed would be callous and would endanger the future of the sport.

If, however, you wish to find out more of the rich heritage and background to the sport, or want to find out if you are capable of keeping a raptor properly, or if you are already a falconer and are keen to learn more, then read on. Whichever category you fit into, I hope you enjoy the book. I will try to explain the falconry terms as I go, however a quick glimpse at the Glossary should be of assistance while you familiarize yourself with them.

The weathering lawn at The English School of Falconry. Proprietor Phil Gooden holds aloft a Tawny Eagle.

1 THE ESSENCE OF FALCONRY

Falconry is a sport that lends itself to the romantically inclined. No-one really knows where or when it originated, although it is believed to have first been practised in the Far East around 4,000 years ago. Its true origins are probably even further back, however, lost in the swirling mists of time.

What is more certain is *why* falconry started. Someone, somewhere was watching a bird of prey stoop and catch its quarry with what must have seemed like enviable ease and monotonous regularity. Then, the eureka moment of thought that all falconers should be ever-grateful for: why could the bird not do that for a human master and thus provide a supply of food for the dinner table? In those days, man's chances of catching food were limited by strength, stamina, and the ability to construct tricky traps or weapons. So the idea of a 'tame' bird of prey doing the work on their behalf must have been tempting indeed.

Everything the sport is today springs from that precise moment, and, incredible as it may seem, very little has changed in terms of technique and practice since those distant days. There have, of course, been pivotal developments that ease the task immensely, and modern materials and engineering processes have overcome many problems. But, fundamentally, falconry is the same sport it was 4,000 years ago, and the basic aim remains the same: using a trained bird to catch live quarry in its natural habitat.

Nowadays, there is not such a life-or-death need to catch food for the table, so falconry is practised for its heritage and for the undeniable thrill it still offers. Ideally, newcomers to the sport should invest in a day's hawking at one of the established centres (see Useful Addresses). The experience is unforgettable and will reveal one way or the other whether falconry is for you.

LOVE AT FIRST SIGHT

I first experienced hawking when I was sent along to The English School of Falconry in Buckinghamshire to write a feature for the newspaper on which I was working at the time.

Prior to this I had always had a passion for birds, and as a youngster had taken the time and effort to learn how to identify the different species, especially those I particularly liked, such as the corvids (crow family) and birds of prey. At a more tender age I had briefly dallied with the idea of taking up falconry and obtaining a buzzard *(Buteo buteo)* after seeing a trade stall at a county show, but in the end I caught the shooting bug which kept me occupied for most of my formative years. As a result I spent hours on end in the countryside in all weather conditions and at all times of the day and night, and so utilized my knowledge of birds and learned a lot more about the natural world.

For those early years, I will always be thankful to my father; his love of all things wild was passed on to me and I remember listening enthralled to his tales of life on a Buckinghamshire farm shortly after the Second World War. His family lived off 'the fat of the land', and stories of dogs and ferrets, guns and country were manna to a youngster like me, hungry for knowledge about the British countryside and beyond. Together, we enjoyed early forays into the frosty morning, armed with one gun between us. More often than not, we returned home empty-handed (for which I continually blamed him for being a poor shot).

It was around my fourteenth birthday that I was finally allowed an airgun of my own and went out hunting alone for the first time. Before I finally gave up shooting many years later I had progressed to

Phil Gooden – with the omnipresent roll up.

shotguns and rifles and was quite a shot. My fieldcraft skills had also improved considerably and they were put to good use spying on some of nature's more wary wildlife without the intent to shoot it.

Over the years my fascination with birds of prey remained undiminished, and I had already encountered a few while out on my forays; mainly kestrels, for they were in plentiful supply in my part of the world, but I had also come across the more elusive sparrowhawk, and, most memorable of all, the mighty buzzard. The latter was encountered on a shooting trip to Devon. I had never seen such a huge bird, as in those days I lived in the wrong part of the country to spot them. I am pleased to report that the buzzard continues to do well in the wild and in those

same fields where I once strolled with my gun under my arm, I can now stand and watch buzzards wheel overhead.

By the time I was assigned to write the aforementioned feature on The English School of Falconry, my shooting days were over. My love of wildlife was undiminished, however, and when I stepped from my car and heard those exotic bird cries coming from the weathering lawn, my heart rate increased a little. There was the unmistakable cry of the redtail hawk, which can be heard on countless cowboy and Indian movies, echoing around the dusty hillsides as our hero cowers behind a boulder; the outraged squawk of a harris hawk; the evocative, plaintive mew of a buzzard; and the harsh and expectant 'kek-kek-kek' of a peregrine. These same sounds have a similar effect on me now.

In the morning (and it was one of those cold, dank ones if I remember rightly) we were taken out with a posse of juvenile harrises. They spent most of their time squawking and squabbling with each other, but I was utterly spellbound. The photographer on the assignment, my old partner Andy Keech, had soon had enough and headed back to the warmth of the newsroom. I told him to tell the News Editor not to expect me back. I was having a whale of a time!

The proprietor, Phil Gooden, had more than forty years' experience of the sport, and a lot of tales to tell, and he told each one with gusto, emphasized by a hearty laugh. I soaked up the atmosphere as the stories rolled on.

We headed out into the countryside armed with an old hand, Mojo, a big and stroppy female harris who is still with Phil some years later. She proved deadly that afternoon and I will never forget watching her as she folded her wings and stooped at a steep angle from an overhead power cable into a scrub of common hawthorn. The sheer ferocity of it was breathtaking, then all hell broke loose as Mojo crashed through the undergrowth with her prize – a woodpigeon which had been tucked up out of the wind. Peering through the fence wire and parting the scrub, I saw her mantling over the already dead pigeon. She was magnificent, every feather bristling, her breast heaving from her exertions. With a glare that dared me to come any closer, she bent her head and began to feed on the warm flesh.

My write-up in the following week's regional paper was ecstatic, and eventually I gave up my day job so that I could spend more time with the birds. I was hooked. Falconry is one of those passions that grabs you and never lets go. You cannot do it half-heartedly. It is an all-pervading enigma that is uppermost in your brain when you wake and the last thing on your mind as you drift off to sleep at night.

THE HISTORY OF FALCONRY

This strange power of appeal has meant that falconry has grown at a fast pace, attracting more and more followers. Even today among the steppe and mountains of Mongolia or Russia, falconry in its most primeval (and often brutal) forms is still practised. Eagles (often golden or tawnies) are caught and hand-reared and taught to chase and catch wolves. It is a fearsome sight to see.

Falconry was practised by learned ancient Egyptians and Chinese as early as 2000BC, and across the East throughout Arabia, India, Japan and beyond long before the Christians arrived. Europe seems to have first dipped its collective toe in the waters of the sport around 300BC, and Britain seems to have discovered it during the reign of the Saxon King Ethelbert (AD860–865). It caught on very quickly and was boosted by the return to the country of the Crusaders, who injected new and exciting training methods and birds they had obtained from the East.

It was not long before the nobility were exchanging their best falcons as a mark of esteem and status. Not for the landed gentry the dowdier hunting birds used to catch a rabbit for dinner; Kings, Queens and aristocrats around the world took falcons (mainly peregrines and the highly sought-after gyr) into the field to catch such salubrious quarry as herons and red kites. I must admit the thought is a mouth-watering one; imagine the splendour of it all – the nobility surrounded by their servants and their magnificently cared-for birds in some of the finest hunting terrain you can imagine. The birds would be pitted against the wily heron or kite (numbers of both were far above the levels of today and were therefore able to support the sport). The thrill of the chase as spectators on horseback charged through the countryside trying to keep an eye on the deadly duel being played out above their heads must have been spectacular.

Emperor Frederick II of Hohenstaufen was perhaps the greatest of all the grandiose falconers, and one of the aforementioned returning Crusaders. The thirteenth-century ruler was a learned man, and despite his indulgent upbringing dedicated his adult life to learning more about the natural world, in particular birds of prey and their use in falconry. His treatise on the sport, still available if you search hard enough, is as fine a falconry book as you could hope to read. Only occasionally are his observations and practices off the mark. The Emperor even goes as far as offering different opinions on evolution and behaviour to those put forward by famous scholars and recognized experts. Time and advanced scientific study have proved him right on most occasions.

He was a man ahead of his time, and he travelled extensively to learn of other lands and their cultures, always accompanied by his team of full-time falconers. The Emperor was in the enviable position of being able to spend vast periods of his life practising falconry, and so became a master. One of his favourite haunts was a castle in Sicily; a beautiful palace, enriched with statues and furniture extolling the virtues of his obsession. From there he would take his finest hawks, sojourn into the Sicilian countryside and spend weeks at a time watching his beloved birds work the cobalt blue sky.

The Emperor's travelling menagerie must have awed European residents as it passed from country to country at will. A vast and bizarre array of birds, reptiles and mammals followed him on his travels, so he could never be far from his learning material. Poverty-stricken peasants in particular must have been impressed by the procession past their humble homes. The 'zoo' even included a giraffe.

Emperor Frederick was, of course, not alone in his passion. Monarchs and noblemen down the ages continued to become hooked on the sport, ensuring its seamless passage through the centuries. When Robert of Avenel granted his lands in Dumfriesshire to the Abbey of Melrose around the twelfth century, he reserved the rights to the falcon nesting sites; Henry II annually sent for falcons from Pembrokeshire from 1173; and King John obtained falcons from County Antrim in 1212–13. The title of Grand Falconer for the country was even created for the Bishop of St Albans. He was paid an annual stipend of £1,000 for the privilege, a tradition only revoked this century. Meanwhile, the lowly peasant continued to use his birds to quietly hunt for the pot and provide for his family.

It was not until the advent of gunpowder and reliable guns that falconry suffered its first major decline in popularity. Why spend time and money on birds and their upkeep when you could simply grab a gun and some shot and head out for a day's sport? The ruling classes had found a new love and falconry

suffered dramatically. It is strange how things come full circle. In Scotland in 1551 it was deemed punishable by death to take game birds, so there were plenty left for falconers; in later days the vitriol was turned against the birds for taking sport from the guns.

The Civil War at the beginning of the seventeenth century was also thought to have had a particularly big impact on the sport's decline. Not only were many of its upper class practitioners removed from the field, the new Puritan regime frowned upon sport in general. Full-time falconers slowly became a thing of the past. Even the loyal peasant, ever faithful to the cause, gradually turned to weapons as their price came down. Guns were easy to use and maintain – and still put dinner on the table.

For a while, it looked as though the days of the sport were numbered. But a hardcore of followers never gave it up and the knowledge passed from generation to generation. The colourful sportsman Colonel Thornton of Yorkshire was a leading participant and, with Lord Orford, formed a Hawking Club sometime around 1775; members rallied and the sport entered the twentieth century with a band of followers keeping its traditions alive and kicking.

The latter half of this century has seen the greatest renaissance of the sport in modern times. Despite the increasing pressure on country sports, falconry is thriving, with an estimated 20,000 practising falconers in the UK and plenty more followers. Thanks to participation by some personality falconers, a wider public is learning about the sport, which can only lead to its greater appreciation. Country issues are suddenly very much on the agenda, and falconers have an enviable history and tradition to their sport, of which they are rightly proud.

Unfortunately, however, falconry has recently had something of a stigma attached to it, as a result of those individuals who call themselves falconers but who are actually nothing more than criminals of the worst kind, profiting from the sale of rare and protected birds and their eggs. Most of the stories about petty thugs selling falcons to wealthy Arabs for vast sums of money are absolute piffle, though not all.

True falconers come from all backgrounds and yet are able to communicate for hours at a time in the way only the obsessed can. Every falconer I know is proud to be one, although at times the frustration of the sport can be enough to test the patience of a saint. There is a superb sense of camaraderie in the sport, marred only by those who cannot help boasting about their birds and making outrageous statements about what quarry it regularly takes.

A friend of mine tackled one of the 'my bird's better than yours' brigade when we were caught by him while out hawking one day. Straight away we knew he was telling lies. He told us he was flying a peregrine–saker hybrid, and when we asked him what it flew at (what weight did the bird perform at), he replied, 'Anything. It takes all sorts: rabbits, hares, pigeons, gulls. It's had them all. It's really quick.'

We looked at each other resignedly. The wonder-falconer then started to describe another bird he had, this one a pure saker, big as a goose, and so on . . . The sun was lowering and we were keen to get on with the hawking and get our birds home. His patience finally worn out, my mate nodded at the newcomer's dog, a scruffy old mongrel. 'I suppose he brings down elephants does he?' he inquired politely. It did the trick.

FALCONRY DEMONSTRATIONS

One aspect of falconry that gets particularly bad press is the demonstration team, of which there are several in the country of varying standards.

Some purists claim that these displays are a bastardization of the sport and should be stopped. In

Falconry displays – good education or a pure money-spinner?

Kestrels are the most common birds of prey in the country, yet many people never even notice them.

When engaged in a dull or arduous task, my thoughts turn to my hawk.

some ways I agree. Poorly done, they give a terrible image of the falconer. If the birds are ill-treated, unkempt and untrained, who can blame the general public for thinking we do not give a damn about the birds? On the other hand, a well-choreographed, entertaining and educational display is a delight to watch. Unfortunately, the latter is rare. Nevertheless, the good done by these displays does, I think, outdo the bad. At least the public can come close to these magnificent creatures and learn about them and their habitat.

I am continually astonished – and increasingly concerned – at how little both adults and children know about their own countryside. Once, when helping out at an activity day at The English School

of Falconry, I was showing one paying guest a juvenile female kestrel we had been training.

'Ooh,' he said, 'what a lovely bird. Where does that come from?'

I informed him it was an indigenous species, and was actually very common.

'Well, I have never seen one of those in my life, I had no idea they were around!' he exclaimed.

The man was a sales rep, and travelled thousands of miles a year up and down the country's motorways. He probably passed half-a-dozen kestrels every day and yet he had never actually seen one.

If a single demonstration makes a single child go home and look in a bird book to learn more about the barn owl he has just handled, haven't we achieved something worthy? Ashley Smith at the Hawk Conservancy in Andover has an excellent method of instilling learning; youngsters are more than welcome to have their picture taken with a bird of prey – as long as they promise to go home and read up about it afterwards.

Falconry, then, is simply described in theory, but is far more subtle upon closer inspection. By means of an introduction, it is probably useful to tell you that, traditionally, hawking is carried out in the winter, and the birds are 'stood down' (not flown) during the summer so they can moult out properly. This is discussed in greater detail in Chapter 4.

The attractions of falconry are many and varied, although hard to describe to those with little or no interest in the natural world around them. Suffice to say, whenever I am engaged in a dull or arduous task, I turn my mind to my hawk. What is he doing now in his weathering? Preening, watching a speck in the sky, or calling for me? Is he on flying weight, too high, too low? Is he fit and healthy? The list is endless. Often, I look out of a window while I am absorbed by these thoughts, and if it is a clear and sunny winter morning, my heart sinks even lower. There is no doubt in my mind where I would rather be. The answer is always the same: standing on a lonely hillside on my favourite hawking ground, overlooking a valley of varied terrain, all of which I have permission to fly over. The wind is in my face which is upturned watching Archie, my harris hawk, soar above. There is nothing stopping him from disappearing into the blue; nothing but that intangible bond between us that is the very essence of falconry.

2 BIRDS OF PREY USED IN FALCONRY

There are two main categories of birds of prey used in falconry: longwings and shortwings. You will notice that I give the weights of some of these birds to demonstrate the sort of size and power they possess. These are approximate weights; they should not be taken as models on which to train individual birds. Each bird is different and has a different flying weight.

A classic longwing stoop.

LONGWINGS

The longwings are the true falcons. They have long, tapered, scythe-like wings, swept back from their bodies, which allow them a fast turn of speed and the ability to cut through the air. Falcons are mainly aerial combatants; they take a lot of birds and are well equipped for knocking them out of the sky. The prey is either killed outright by a lethal blow to the neck or spine as the falcon flashes down from above, or it is pounced upon and the spinal cord transected

with a neat twist of the bill. Falcons have a small notch or tooth on their beak which locks into the vertebrae of their prey; a quick twist and the quarry is dispatched.

Falcons are among the noblest of falconry birds. Their sheer speed and agility is enough to get the crowds 'oohing' at displays, and their nonchalance while sitting on their block is beguiling. Traditionally, falcons are flown at rooks in open country and at grouse on moorland. More recently, some success has been had in what I would call 'walked-up' hawking – simply a hedgerow hunt with a falcon waiting on above. The term 'falconer' was originally reserved just for those who flew falcons; those who flew hawks were known as austringers. The term is now generally used to describe both activities.

THE PEREGRINE
(Falco peregrinus) Female: 1lb 14oz to 2lb 3oz; Male: 1lb 3oz to 1lb 7oz

For centuries regarded as *the* falconry bird, the peregrine is still widely used today, although the reduction in open, unobstructed tracts of land has dealt it a severe blow. Much nonsense has been written about the peregrine and the speed of its impressive stoop. Estimates have put it at upwards of 200mph, but whatever the speed, it is a brutally effective means of catching prey.

In the 1950s and 1960s, the use of the chemical DDT in farming nearly finished this magnificent bird off. The chemical was so persistent that it stayed in the food chain, and eventually made its way to the top – and the peregrine. This had a disastrous effect on the bird's breeding capability. It affected the amount of calcium the female peregrines could produce and therefore the eggs laid had pathetically thin shells. They simply kept breaking in the nest. Fortunately, the link was discovered in time and the pesticide was banned.

The number of peregrines has increased dramatically since then, to such an extent that pigeon fanciers are now calling for action to limit them once more. It is claimed the raptors are killing so many prize pigeons en route to their homes that the sport is becoming impossible. There is also pressure from game managers. Moorland game birds are apparently suffering as a result of the increase in peregrine numbers and owners are now calling for controls. The Royal Society for the Protection of Birds argues otherwise. It says the number of peregrines is only now reaching the level it should be at – and suggests that pigeon fanciers devise methods to avoid putting the birds into the firing line.

Many falconers suffer from 'peregrinitis'. In other words, if you do not fly a peregrine, you are not worthy of calling yourself a falconer. This is, of course, utter nonsense, and it is usually the self-same people who take on peregrines when they should not, making a very poor job of it at best and, more probably, losing their falcon.

Longwings generally, but peregrines in particular, need large areas of open land because of their methods of hunting. In the wild, they traverse many square miles of cliff face and estuary, using sea winds to fire them at speed across the sky. When they eventually do stoop at quarry, whether it be a feral pigeon or wader, they time their attack so their victim is out in the open with little or no available cover. Once 'put in' (hiding in cover) the wild peregrine's victim is lost.

A similar terrain is needed for a trained peregrine. In enclosed country the bird will be lost from sight quickly as it quarters for food. You may well have fitted it with a telemetry clip so you can follow the signal and hopefully find it again, but over-reliance on telemetry is not falconry.

In the days of the Old Hawking Club, which was the last to employ full-time falconers in this country, Salisbury Plain was the bastion of good peregrine territory. There the bird came into its own as a rook hawk (see Chapter 7). During the game season, peregrines were also widely used as fine grouse birds, tearing from the sky at tremendous speed and

knocking quarry out of the air. It is a rare bird indeed that can adapt to both rook and grouse hawking.

LANNER FALCON

(Falco biarmicus) Female: 1lb 4oz to 1lb 10oz; Male: 14oz to 1.2oz

Probably the most popular falcon in the sport today, due in no small part to its use as the central figure in most bird-of-prey demonstrations. These falcons can vary enormously in their performance; some may fly very poorly, while others will put the best showbirds to shame. They have a mixed reputation as hunting birds, again because of the apparent inconsistency in their performance. They are generally regarded as too small to tackle grouse, and show little inclination to tackle tough old rooks. They have come into their own, however, as suppliers of a more relaxed type of longwing flying, the equivalent of rough shooting. Being opportunists, the lanner can be flown in hedgerow country, turning over quickly and dropping on any flushed quarry below.

In the wild, the lanner is a versatile and successful predator, resident in steppe territory, woodland, moorland, mountain, wetlands and coastal regions throughout parts of Europe, North Africa and the Middle East. Because of its varied habitat, the lanner is used to most weather conditions, although one has to be careful of frostbite (see Chapter 4).

It feeds on birds, caught on the ground and in the air, and reptiles. A cast of lanners can be successfully deployed, as is proved in the wild when a mated pair make hunting look easy. And occasionally, when waterhole conditions are right, twenty or more lanners tolerate each other and hunt side by side. Only when resources thin out do they return to their more normal, solitary lifestyle. The male is known as a lanneret.

SAKER

(Falco cherrug) Female: 1lb 15oz to 2lb 3oz; Male: 1lb 6oz to 1lb 10oz

Renowned as a difficult bird, the saker needs a lot of work if it is to succeed. Again, some individuals excel, while others show no more prowess than 'straight-lining' – literally setting off in one direction and continuing into the wild blue yonder. This can

The ever-versatile lanner.

Saker – the bird of the desert.

be explained in part by their seemingly overriding migration instinct. During August, September and again in April and May, wild saker populations are on the move, and even captive-bred birds are likely to join them if allowed free. This therefore takes a big chunk out of your potential training/flying time, and even then the results are dependent on whether or not you have picked a normal saker or a bird of wilder temperament.

They have trouble with the wind, being big birds, but are determined to succeed and therefore venture to the very limits of what could be called controlled hawking. Sakers, being birds of more arid conditions, are also prone to waterlogging, further hampering flight. Their feathers soak up a good deal of water, like a sponge, the result being that your saker is likely to fly like a sponge as well.

The saker is the staple falconry bird of the Middle East. It is taken as a passage bird (a wild bird already flying and hunting for itself) and is trained for use against such desert-dwelling quarry as the houbara. This bird, a kind of bustard or heron, is apparently in decline due in no small part to the attentions of overzealous falconers and their sakers. Indeed, the situation looks unlikely to improve, for Middle Eastern falconers (like the rest of us) have become obsessed with their sport. Those wealthy participants in oil-rich countries spend vast amounts of time and money on it. Pick-up trucks are specially adapted to accommodate both hawks and the watching party, and when a houbara is spotted, the bird is unhooded. Then, a wild, high-speed chase follows as the bird pursues the fast houbara among the desert scrub. The four-wheel-drive vehicle and occupants try to follow as fast as possible up and down the sand dunes (a memorable account of this can be found at the end of Philip Glasier's unsurpassable *Falconry and Hawking* (Batsford)). This sounds an exciting pastime, but one which seems likely to mean the end of the poor houbara if continued.

In the wild the saker can be found mainly on steppe, moorland and mountain terrain, passaging through semi-arid woodland. The main quarry of wild sakers is mammalian, in particular susliks in steppe grassland; the saker flies low over the ground hoping to surprise the suslik, a type of ground squirrel. It also takes small birds and reptiles such as lizards and frogs. The male is sometimes referred to as a sakret.

LUGGER FALCON

(Falco jugger) Similar size to saker

Not appreciated by most falconers due to its entirely unpredictable nature. As an example, trying to get a lugger to sit on the fist can remain a major trial weeks after training has begun.

Again, like the saker, they are prone to waterlogging, particularly as juveniles. For most purposes, the trusty lanner excels the larger lugger, although some individuals do eventually prove themselves after perseverance from the falconer.

GYR FALCON

(Falco rusticolus) Female: 2lb 13oz to 3lb 9oz; Male: 2lb to 2lb 10oz

The gyr is the archetypal falcon of old, and even today is one of the most desirable – and therefore expensive.

The gyr is a big, powerful falcon, significantly bigger than the others and breathtakingly fast, however no concrete results seem to have been achieved by UK falconers using this most special of birds. Although many have been tried at grouse, few have succeeded in proper style, due in part to the gyr's favoured hunting method: an all-out flat sprint rather than a stooping blow from above. Used to temperatures associated with the Arctic tundra, the gyr can suffer in warmer climes, particularly with respiratory illnesses.

The gyr's disposition is suited to its status; it does not suffer fools gladly and can be a frustrating partner. Its penchant for straight-line hunting also means it is likely to be considered lost more often than most. Do not expect to fly a gyr in enclosed territory without it disappearing over the horizon.

In the wild, the gyr is resident in taiga (coniferous forests in the northern hemisphere). Because of its size, it needs a larger hunting territory than most; incredibly this may be as much as 500sq km. Its prey consists of medium-sized birds, mostly taken on or near the ground. It may not kill daily, but feed upon a kill for up to a week. Males are attractively called jerkins.

PRAIRIE FALCON

(Falco mexicanus) Weight not reliably tested in the UK
Beloved by American falconers, the prairie is rarely seen on UK shores. An aggressive little bird, it has proved too lightweight to tackle our traditional winter fare of rook or grouse, and is not adept at more enclosed walked-up hawking either.

MERLIN

(Falco columbarius) Slightly smaller than sparrowhawk (see page 25)
Not as prevalent as in former days when this delightful little falcon was used primarily to take the lark. Today this may not seem a very politically correct pastime, but when the gorgeous skylark was omnipresent in our fields and meadows, these falcons provided what must have been some of the very finest hawking on offer.

Lark hawking is the style that best reflects the type of flight known as 'ringing up', because this is exactly what the lark does to escape a pursuer; it climbs higher and higher in the sky in small circles at an impressive pace. The dedicated merlin will respond in like fashion and an incredible aerial duel will follow. Both birds can climb so high they become invisible to the naked eye, then plummet earthwards with the lark seeking refuge in vegetation and the falcon hot on his heels. A friend of mine was lucky enough to witness such a flight and kindly recounted the following to give us a flavour of the experience:

It was a glorious day, without a cloud in the sky, and we were ambling down into a meadow when Cherry (the merlin) tore off after a skylark. The lark at first did not appear unduly bothered and began to climb steadily. As Cherry closed he seemed to change down a gear and the pair began to ring up, something I had never seen before. I leant back against a nearby field maple and, shading my eyes from the sun, watched as the pair continued to rise into the blue in sweeping, purposeful circles. Eventually, they were just a speck in the sky, and then, suddenly, they were gone. All there was to be seen was an expanse of blue sky. Minutes passed and I must admit we exchanged worried glances; Cherry could have disappeared anywhere by now. Then suddenly my friend spotted a black dot screaming down from the sky. The lark came first, hotly pursued by Cherry who was occasionally stooping at him. The little bird was jinking aside at the last minute while still heading for the ground at terrific speed. Just when it seemed both birds would be dashed to pieces in the grassland before our very eyes, the lark dived into a clump of tall grass and nettles. Cherry, knowing she was beaten, threw up and, with a lap of honour, returned to the fist. It was only then I remembered to breathe once more. It was quite the most spectacular flying display I have ever been privileged to witness.

These days, you need a special licence from the Department of the Environment to take larks, and you are also hard pressed to find them in significant numbers. It is still possible, however, under the right circumstances, and must rank as one of the most rewarding of flights.

Merlins are traditionally flown as a pair or cast. In the wild, merlins specialize in small birds which they snatch in direct flight. The male is known as a jack.

HOBBY

(Falco subbuteo) Similar size to merlin
Like the kestrel, this bird has no real use for the serious falconer as it catches little more than insects and small birds. But these pretty birds can be found in bird-of-prey centres and at the occasional display. The hobby is known for its speciality of catching dragonflies and casually eating them limb by limb while still on the wing. The hobby will also take bats and small birds – at least seventy species of small birds have been recorded in the hobby's diet – and is crepuscular, meaning it hunts mainly at dawn or dusk.

KESTREL

(Falco tinnunculus) Similar size to sparrowhawk
The beloved kestrel, known to many for its habit of hovering low near roads and motorways, used to be a beginner's bird in falconry, but thankfully this idea seems to have been lost over time. Except for educational use in a falconry display, the kestrel has no part to play in modern falconry and should certainly never be handed into the care of an inexperienced falconer.

In terms of taking quarry, the trained kestrel shows

A magnificent bird in top plumage kept in quality surroundings should be the aim of every falconer.

The kestrel is an endearing and fascinating falcon, but it has no place in falconry.

little interest, unless you are keen on adding lists of beetles, mice and the occasional earthworm to your hawking diary. Because it is such a small bird, any substantial changes in bodyweight are likely to affect the bird a great deal. Therefore, a novice unsure of how much weight to take off a bird could quite easily kill it within hours. On cold nights, that half an ounce less could be the death of the bird.

In the wild, the kestrel appears to be doing well, so much so that in some parts of the country it is unusual to travel in the countryside without seeing at least one. Indeed, on one of my own hawking grounds, a pair are regularly in attendance and lose no opportunity to 'buzz' Archie, my male harris hawk, despite the vast difference in size. Wild birds feed mainly on insects and small mammals such as voles and mice. They also catch worms and lizards

and will take small birds, mainly during the breeding season when young and incautious songbirds are plentiful. Males have a slate-grey hood, females do not.

HYBRIDS

Hybrid falcons now seem to be all the rage; if you do not have a gyr-cross-peregrine, you are simply not worth your salt among some groups of falconers.

But the interbreeding of species does have its downside, as well as picking up the benefits of either bird. Many hybrids have proved unmanageable or particularly lethargic, while others have proved susceptible to disease. On the other hand, there have been some successes, notably the pere–lanner combination, which not only produces a good, powerful working bird, but a nice-looking one too.

Other combinations have resulted in promising birds, so hybridization should not be totally abhorred. However, there are some who say the art of falconry is being degraded by the continued experimentation with nature's lines of evolution.

SHORTWINGS

The classic shortwing outline, displaying splayed primaries that prevent stalling at slow speeds.

TRUE HAWKS

The true hawks, the goshawk and sparrowhawk, are superbly adapted for forest-dwelling killers. Their short, rounded wings and manoeuvrable tails help them steer and swerve through the trees at astounding speed. They kill, like buzzards, with their feet, pinning their prey with needle-sharp talons and crushing them in their vice-like grip.

THE GOSHAWK

(Accipiter gentilis) Female: 2lb to 2lb 10oz; Male: 1lb 4oz to 1lb 9oz

The goshawk has long been regarded as the ultimate hunting bird. The range of quarry this ferocious hunter will take is astounding; from songbirds to corvids (crow family), rats to hares, the gos will take them all with aplomb. Startlingly quick from the fist

or from overhead, the gos overpowers its prey by sheer speed in flat-out flight, then uses its big feet and powerful talons to dispatch it.

Arguably the greatest challenge a falconer can face, many a gos has been lost due to inexperienced handling. This bird needs manning sessions every day; if it is not at least handled daily, it returns to an almost wild state surprisingly quickly – a hissing, spitting merchant of doom. Goshawks are tetchy, irascible characters, and as such are prone to sudden impulsive fits of rage. They can bate themselves into the ground and apparently suffer from aneurysms. Their nervous disposition means they have to be flown at exactly the right weight to be successful, and again I reiterate that only the most experienced of falconers should take one on.

In the wild, the gos is the top of the food chain, although extremely difficult to see. It takes large, strong quarry with consummate ease; pheasants, squirrels, crows, pigeons, rabbits and jays all regularly form part of its diet. The female, as in most birds of prey, is considerably larger than her mate and is therefore capable of tackling the larger quarry. Although resembling the sparrowhawk in appearance, the gos is bigger. Most confusion is caused by wrongly identifying a male gos as a female sparrowhawk.

Pine forests are this bird's favourite. Strangely enough, the wild population seems to have actually prospered at the hands of falconers. While rogue 'falconers' have been robbing nests for years, it appears that escaped goshawks have enabled effective reintroduction and breeding in some areas. Still a rare bird, but apparently numbers are on the increase.

SPARROWHAWK

(Accipiter nisus) Female: 7oz to 10oz; Male: 4.5oz to 7oz

The spar is a clever little hunter, utilizing cover ingeniously to get close to prey before flicking over the hedge at speed and plucking the unsuspecting bird from the ground. Indeed, this bird has even been seen running between ground cover before taking to the wing to surprise its quarry.

Many urban residents are amazed when they see this fierce-eyed predator in their gardens. Bird tables

The goshawk; the true austringer's bird.

have become a favourite ambush point, and because spars have a penchant for favourite 'plucking posts', residents may also be treated to a display of the bird plucking and devouring its meal nearby.

The sparrowhawk was a popular bird in falconry in the past, and a pair were thought a particularly effective method of pinning down magpies. Believe it or not, the bird used to be given added impetus when quarry was spotted by being thrown like a dart by the falconer. Apparently, the bird does not mind this at all, although I wouldn't fancy trying the trick with anything larger! The male is known as a musket.

BROADWINGS

BUZZARDS

Many people refer to the buzzard-type birds of prey as broadwings, and classify them in the same group as eagles because of their distinctive shape and method of flight.

Buzzards are a classic shape that we would all recognize as being especially 'hawklike'. They have big, coloured eyes, often orange or yellow, bright yellow ceres (the waxy patch around their beak) and feet, and a rounded, eagle-like beak (the term 'aquiline' used to describe a person's nose comes from the Latin name for eagles – *Aquila*). The eyes are protected from the sun by beetling brows, which provide a hood against the fiercest glare. They also give the bird an unnerving ferocity when it fixes you with an inscrutable gaze.

The buzzard family kills by crushing with incredibly powerful feet, while long, needle-sharp talons grip and skewer the unfortunate prey. Instead of being mainly aerial predators, the buzzards take much of their prey on the ground, soaring high above the earth on thermals and using their incredible eyesight to spot potential prey and then plan an attack route.

Again, these birds are intelligent hunters and successful in evolution terms, although man has persecuted them for their fondness for game birds. Even the buzzard family's liking for carrion has endangered it; many farmers seeing the birds

scavenging from sheep carcasses have wrongly assumed it is the birds doing the killing and have shown them no mercy.

Instead of the long, sharp wings of the falcon, the buzzards have broad, rounded wings with particularly pronounced primary feathers (the outsplayed feathers that look like fingers on the wingtips). These help the birds make the most of their speed without simply stalling and dropping from the sky.

BUZZARD
(Buteo buteo) Similar in bulk to a harris hawk
The classic buzzard shape and design, the common buzzard is a lovely bird of mountain and field. Many of you will have marvelled at these big birds as they wheel above in the sky, their plaintive mewing call echoing peacefully around the countryside.

In my youth, trips to Devon and Cornwall were especially welcome, because one was bound to spot a buzzard on a roadside telegraph pole or gliding out of sight as the car passed. Sojourns to one particular Somerset haunt will always stay with me. My parents and I used to spend hours over afternoon cream tea in a lovely old farmhouse in the heart of rolling hillside watching a pair of buzzards on the soar perhaps a mile or so away.

An incredibly successful species, the buzzard has remained rare or even unseen in some parts due to man's fear of its hunting prowess. Many young buzzards are shot, however, and still more are poisoned, even though both practices are illegal.

The buzzard's diet is wide to say the least; one of its mainstays is young rabbits. There is something utterly captivating about finding a favourite buzzard hunting ground and watching a pair at work. Despite their appearance as carefree, casual birds, they can put in a tasty stoop to grab three-quarter grown rabbits and sweep them away. Such is their reliance on rabbits that when the coney population was decimated by the introduction of myxamatosis (some estimate 99 per cent of the UK rabbit population was wiped out by the disease), buzzard numbers plummeted. Fortunately the rabbit survived and so did the buzzard, due in no small part to its flexible eating habits. Like a giant thrush, buzzards can be seen running around pasture and

Hawking on a chilly winter morning with an immature harris.

pulling earthworms out of the ground – a bizarre sight! They are also very keen on carrion and will take rotting sheep carcass any day if it saves them from hunting themselves. Numerous other species including lizards, insects and small birds are also taken.

In falconry terms, the buzzard is the successor to the kestrel as the recommended first bird for beginners. This is not necessarily ideal, for although most buzzards do have fairly accommodating natures, they are inherently lazy and require a lot of hard work and weeks of regular flying before they take quarry with any degree of authority. Many novices may lose patience when they do not see results, and the poor buzzard will get the blame.

HARRIS HAWK

(Parabuteo unicinctus) Female: 2lb to 2lb 6oz; Male: 1lb 3oz to 1lb 9oz

The praises of the harris hawk have been sung above any other bird used in falconry in recent years, and with good reason. I must confess that I too am a convert; these tough little characters have revolutionized the sport and introduced a whole new audience to falconry that would perhaps never have otherwise got involved.

I once wrote in a magazine article that the harris hawk was the labrador of the falconry world. The phrase has stuck and has since been used elsewhere to describe these quirky birds from the USA and South America.

A well-trained harris is a joy to work with; they all have different personality traits, but on the whole they are an amiable bunch. One of the main benefits of harris hawks is that they can be flown as a team. Other birds of prey must be flown singly or in a mated or well-socialized pair; fly more and you risk them killing one another. But because the harris lives in a social group, you can fly a good number together as long as they are socialized with each other. This fact has been exploited by many bird-of-prey centres and display teams. Parties of paying guests can each take charge of a harris hawk for the day and the birds work the fields and hedgerows together as a team.

Younger birds learn a lot from flying with more experienced veterans and exciting flights are guaranteed when the pack sets off at pace after a rabbit or pheasant. With back up, harrises are prepared to tackle large prey, with males even taking hare on occasion. Females can fly at well in excess of 2lb and are a hefty proposition. Males, although lighter, are probably slightly quicker and more nimble. Either way, the range of quarry they have been recorded as taking is remarkably varied, from crows to partridge and beyond.

Although generally regarded as relatively easy birds to train, harris hawks are capable of strange quirks of temperament, with females particularly vulnerable to aggression in adulthood. Mistakes made in training can come back to haunt you, and young birds have a tendency to behave in a very anti-social manner.

My male harris behaved pretty appallingly in his first season, at least in the weathering. He became a screamer, despite the fact that he was around twenty weeks when taken from his seclusion aviary and so could not feasibly be an imprint. Nothing I could do seemed to ease the problem; he screamed whether fed-up or on flying weight. This sort of behaviour is not unusual, particularly with birds kept singly, for they become partly imprinted on the food-provider. Thankfully, most juveniles grow out of this after

Each harris has an undeniable character of its own. Thankfully most are superb companions.

Redtails are good hunters, but notoriously tricky propositions for inexperienced falconers.

their first moult, and even if they do not their voices are far less piercing as adults. You have been warned – consider your neighbours!

Tip: I had some success quieting Archie down by giving him beef bones to pick over. Having virtually no meat on them, there was no danger of him eating too much, but the activity made him forget about squawking for a couple of hours. On the downside, scrabbling about with bones dirties the tail feathers and primaries; the choice is yours!

In the wild, the harris is resident in southern states of the USA and into South America. As I have mentioned, it lives in family packs of several birds and utilizes this fact in hunting like a pride of lions. There have been many harris hawking experiences that have enriched my life, but the following is one I shall never forget:

It was not a pleasant October day for hawking, for the remnants of overnight rain splashed down from the trees above and the breeze was a little too strong for my liking. It was not enough to warrant cancelling the trip, but enough to cause unease whenever Archie lifted off from a swaying branch and followed on. He had only been with me a couple of months and had made remarkable progress from a screaming, terrified youngster to flying completely free and responding to my whistle, but was a little unused to handling the wind.

I walked him down a familiar route through autumnal English countryside. The leaves were not completely off the trees as yet and I had to strain to keep my eye on Archie as he sauntered along, first behind me, then up ahead. He was flying at 1lb 5oz – which should have been just enough to make him keen to grab something. On previous outings he had pounced on two mice and an unfortunate frog and eaten all three in double-quick time, but as yet he was not 'entered', a term falconers use to describe the moment the bird makes its first proper kill. As we made our way around the first big field, Archie contented himself with letting me get in front then flashing up to me, clipping me round the ear with a primary as he flew past and into a tree further on, where he would sit waiting to repeat his party piece. I couldn't see him catching a lot while he continued to play games with me.

We had made it to a line of oak trees bordering my hawking land when a particularly strong gust blew Archie into a tree up ahead and a fresh deluge of rainwater down my neck. I could hear his bells as I waded through soggy grass to get to him and set about searching up the knarled bole for any sign of the daft bird. Again, his bells sounded, and I still couldn't see him, until suddenly an arrowhead of brown and black streaked from one side of the tree to the other and crashed onto a main bough.

Archie's bells were working overtime, but I still couldn't see what he was up to. To be perfectly honest, I thought he was just messing about and catching falling leaves, another of his favourite pastimes.

Then he came fluttering to the ground on the other side of the hedge, obviously mantling some prize in his talons. After much cursing and wrestling with brambles, I too appeared on the other side of the ditch. To my amazement, Archie was delightfully squeezing the life out of a squirrel on the ground. I was concerned because squirrels have a particularly powerful bite and can cause a bird considerable damage. Yet the youngster had pinioned the poor squib by the head and was now proceeding to tuck into this choice meal. Once I was sure the squirrel was dead, I let Archie feed up a little on his first kill. He deserved it. I stood and looked around me and forgot it was wet and cold. At last I could call myself a falconer proper. My bird had been entered – and that was an achievement for both of us.

REDTAIL HAWK/BUZZARD
(Buteo jamaicensis) Female: 2lb 7oz to 3lb; Male: 1lb 6oz to 2lb

The favoured bird of falconers in America, the redtail is a fearsome proposition for any but the most experienced practitioners.

What may seem incongruous is that falconers in the USA start off with a redtail, but unlike their British counterparts, they have already spent years under the tutelage of an experienced falconer before they are allowed anywhere near a live bird. They even have to pass an exam in the sport. It is the general policy that redtails are taken as passage birds, flown for a season and then released back into the wild again. This, of course, would not be an option in the UK; introducing a foreign species is a criminal offence as well as being totally irresponsible.

Redtails need a lot of work and can be temperamental to say the least. A friend of mine was footed twice by an irate female redtail and knew nothing about either strike until he felt the blood flow; both times she went for his eyes. With perseverance, however, the redtail can make an excellent hunting companion, capable of tackling large prey and taking on game birds. They need to be flown regularly to gain any semblance of fitness and can easily 'go back' – if they are left unattended for any length of time, they can take a considerable turn for the worse.

In the wild, the redtail is best known for that beautifully evocative cry; listen carefully to the next western on TV and there is every chance you will hear the sound echoing round the canyons.

FERRUGINOUS BUZZARD

(Buteo regalis) Female: 3lb 8oz to 3lb 12oz; Male: 2lb 2oz to 2lb 5oz

Also known as the ferruginous eagle, this big bird has had mixed results in falconing terms.

The females can be huge, as big as small eagles and capable of tackling decent-sized prey. But while they have famously large gapes and are capable of scoffing large meals before the falconer has a chance to intervene, the ferrugi's feet are diminutive, somewhat hampering their potential.

Their hunting style is not entirely suited to British terrain. In their native North America they hunt on or near the ground, setting off and bearing down on their prey with heavy, remorseless wing beats. Notoriously difficult to man, the ferrugi can become exasperating to the uninitiated. Although useful as a rabbiting bird in open terrain, British falconers have had only limited success with them.

EAGLES

Eagles have recently been classed as broadwings for obvious reasons. They have many buzzard-like tendencies, and most have the classic buzzard look. They range in size from surprisingly small birds to the astonishingly large, and very few have been successfully utilized for hawking purposes, due in part to their wariness of man and increasing scarcity in the wild.

GOLDEN EAGLE

(Aquila chrysaetos)

The classic eagle, and the one found nesting in the upper reaches of Britain and the wilder regions of the Continent, the goldie is a magnificent creature and truly the king of birds.

Females can be awesomely big, weigh a colossal amount, and boast a wing span of around 7ft. A bird that large can, and has, caused considerable damage to careless falconers. Phil Gooden needed thirty-nine stitches in his wrist when he was distracted while feeding a goldie and was 'footed'. If you think an irate harris hurts, take a look at a golden eagle's feet; they are as big as a man's hands.

There are hardly any falconers left now who hunt successfully (note that word) with goldies. Special support braces are necessary for carrying these brutes up and down the vast expanse of uninhabited territory needed to fly them fairly. Do not forget that in the wild goldies must have a hunting territory of around 50sq miles. An eagle is therefore easily lost just because it decides to stretch its wings and zip over the next hill two miles away. In a day's hunting, a goldie is more than capable of travelling hundreds of miles.

Their hunting technique is classic; watching from a crag until they spy some far-off creature with their incredible eyesight, they swoop low, hugging the contours of the land and using natural cover to approach, then put on a devastating burst of speed to overhaul their surprised target. Alternatively, they utilize the wind and thermals to soar, keeping high enough in the sky to avoid detection but allowing themselves a vast tract of land over which to scan for food. Much nonsense has been written and spoken about eagles trying to take off with fully grown deer, babies, and so on, but it is entirely possible that goldies will tackle young red deer and even foxes if times are hard. Nevertheless, the staple food for these glorious predators is the more tame hare or grouse.

BONELLI'S EAGLE

(Hieraateus pennatus)

The bonelli's has been flown in the UK with some success. It is a big, impressive bird, very much like a huge goshawk in appearance. Flying from the fist, or

The ferruginous buzzard. Note the extraordinary gape.

Like a monstrous goshawk, the bonelli's eagle is an impressive bird. Note the thick, strong legs and massive feet.

encouraged to slope soar above, the bonelli's is more than capable of tackling hare in fine style. It is also an adaptable and versatile bird in the wild, taking a variety of prey on the ground and in the air. It is a habitual hunter, returning to the same grounds each day to quarter and search for food.

Very few of these arid woodland hunters are owned by falconers in the UK and they are therefore expensive when they do come up in collections.

TAWNY EAGLE (Aquila rapax) and STEPPE EAGLE (Aquila nipalensis)
These birds are so similar that some ornithologists have classed one as a sub-species of the other. For actual hunting purposes, these birds have little to offer. The tawny is a piratical thief, stealing food from others (hence its Latin name being so similar to 'rapacious'?). It also spends much of its time scavenging carrion, and used to enjoy colonial shooting parties; injured and dead birds were an easy meal for it to snaffle.

The Steppe also has a liking for carrion, but amazingly for such a big bird, it spends a large amount of time raiding termite nests.

Other eagle species do crop up in collections and displays, but could not be called falconry birds in the strictest sense.

3 FALCONRY FURNITURE

The different (and very specialized) types of equipment used in falconry are traditionally termed furniture. This general term covers just about everything used in the day-to-day management of your bird.

SCALES

The most important part of the falconer's furniture are his scales; without these, he can never be really sure of his hawk's true condition, and may even endanger her life.

The traditional set of falconry scales is the old-fashioned kitchen variety, with a plate for weights on one side and a receptacle on the other. These can be easily adapted to suit your purpose; remove the weighing dish on one side, and depending on the kind of cradle it sits on, decide how you can best put a perch in place. My perch is simply a piece of broomhandle cut to length and covered with a thin strip of carpet. This gives the hawk something to grip and is less cold/slippery than bare wood. My perch is detachable and is attached merely by two notches cut in the underside of the broomhandle. The cradle spokes wedge into these notches, providing a secure base, but the perch can be removed if necessary.

Old-fashioned lead weights should be used to establish the weight of your bird (it is advisable to have all weights from 2lb down to ¼oz, if possible). The additional weight of the perch can be offset by placing weights underneath it to ensure it balances. Otherwise, you will have to start adding and subtracting ounces to make up the difference, a time-consuming and potentially dangerous practice should your maths be wrong.

Tip: make sure the lead weights you purchase are indeed the correct weight; they can be astoundingly inaccurate, so check them on a reliable scale elsewhere.

Brand new, these scales cost around £30, however the lead weights are hard to find and very expensive, perhaps as much as the scales again. Try looking for a secondhand set, and, again, make sure they are accurate before risking the life of your hawk.

Spring-balance scales can be used effectively, but the springs should be checked regularly to ensure continued accuracy. Electronic scales have been mooted as a good buy elsewhere, but I fail to see how even the most placid bird can be asked to stand flat-footed and stock still in order to gain a proper reading. I may well be proved wrong, but the idea seems challenging, for a beginner at least.

HAWKING GLOVE

Another essential piece of furniture is the hawking glove, traditionally an ornate affair of the finest supple leather. The somewhat garish decorations probably stem from a time when the nobility regularly practised the sport and tried to outdo each other on the hawking field. The tassles, embroidery and general handicraft utilized in what is essentially a fairly ordinary working glove are still part of falconry today, although it is not the done thing to go over the top. Some falconers do their very best to look like a medieval king, but sadly end up looking rather silly.

Tip: make sure your glove has a metal loop sewn into it. This is extremely useful for attaching to your belt with the use of a cast metal clip, such as those used

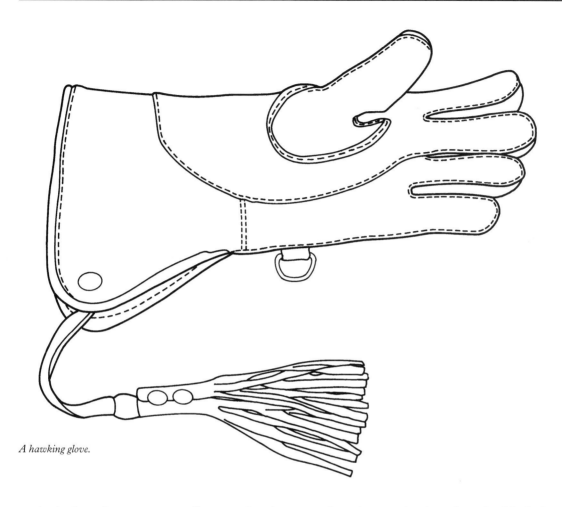

A hawking glove.

on dog leads, and prevents you stuffing your glove in a pocket in a moment of excitement, then discovering it missing minutes later.

The reason for the stoutness of falconry gloves is pure common sense; they have to be thick enough to prevent sharp talons piercing the fist on which the bird sits. During training, falconry birds are scared and wary of man and their natural reaction is to clench their feet, generally not out of malice (with the occasional exception!). A small bird can cause surprisingly excruciating pain by a squeeze on an unprotected wrist; indeed the larger species are capable of causing pain through very thick gauntlets. Even if the dagger-like talons cannot pass through the material, they are quite capable of pinioning one's wrist at four different points and applying incredible pressure. Try pressing a couple of blunt

pencils against your leg through a pair of denim jeans and you will get some idea of the sensation.

Very high-quality leathers are used for gloves these days, such as buckskin, which is wonderfully supple yet immensely strong. Many falconers continue the age-old tradition of making some, or all, of their own furniture, including gloves. This is no small feat, and I will readily confess that I am not one of them. I may well be castigated by other, more proficient falconers than myself for this, but I must be realistic. Those who know me would take great delight in telling you how hopeless I am at anything resembling handiwork.

Patterns for the making of gloves (and other furniture) are readily available in any number of excellent falconry books. Thankfully, however, there are also a number of fine furniture makers who make a living out of their beloved sport. They offer some

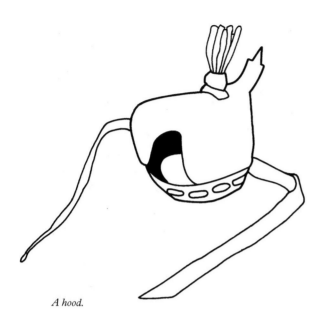

A hood.

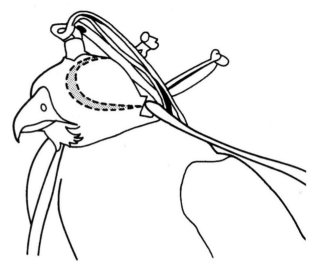

A hooded falcon.

lovely-looking gloves at varying prices, but expect to pay around £50 for a decent glove.

Tip: send an outline of your hand when ordering your glove, as this will ensure a snug fit when the garment arrives. There is nothing worse on a freezing winter's hawking expedition than an ill-fitting gauntlet on one hand.

HOOD

If you intend flying falcons, you will also need a hood. It is used to cover a falcon's vision until it is ready to fly; in this way the bird does not get upset watching another falcon fly while it is tethered. It is advisable to buy one of these, at least at first, as they are devilishly difficult to make. Later, if you are brave enough to try your own, you can learn from some traditional patterns.

TELEMETRY

You would be well advised to invest in some telemetry equipment.

This clever piece of apparatus enables you to attach a radio transmitter to your bird by means of a

lightweight clip fitted to its tail. If the worst happens and she disappears, her whereabouts can be tracked via a hand-held receiver. Telemetry equipment has come down remarkably in price and the quality has also improved since its introduction, but you can still expect to pay several hundred pounds for a good set.

BLOCK/PERCH

Your next consideration should be your bird's perch or block. Traditionally, falcons are kept tethered to blocks, while hawks and buzzards use bow perches. These are supposed to recreate the sort of perch the bird would favour in the wild; generally speaking, you do not find falcons sitting in trees. They are more likely to be found on a cliff face or rocky outcrop, hence the flat-topped block shape. On the other hand, buzzards and hawks are more akin to 'perching birds'. They are likely to be found on branches, hence the bow perch.

Again, the perches can be bought from recognized furniture makers, or the handy falconer (or the one strapped for cash!) can fashion his own. In the old days, a bow perch was made from a suitable piece of wood, either found growing naturally into the right shape at the bottom of a hedgerow, or steamed and bent to fit with a wire base to hold it in place.

A telemetry transmitter (which attaches to the tail) and receiver.

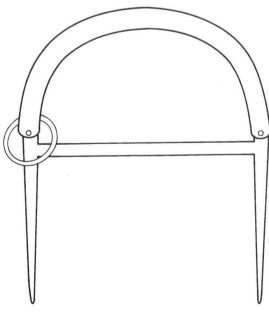

A bow perch.

A ring large enough to pass over the bow must be fitted so that your bird may move around slightly (which she will by bating) and not get her leash tangled, which may result in injury. These days, there are generally two types of bow perch in use: the mobile and the static. The mobile bow perch is exactly the same design as the static, but is fitted with heavy metal plates at the base to weigh it down.

Tip: ensure they *are* heavy weights; it is surprising the size of bow perch that can be dragged by a determined bird. There have been countless examples of this, when hungry birds have bated long enough to get close to another tethered apparently out of reach. The result? One fat bird sitting on the lawn next to a lot of feathers.

The mobile perch can be transported easily, and where no suitable weathering lawn can be found, it can simply be placed on the ground. Static bow

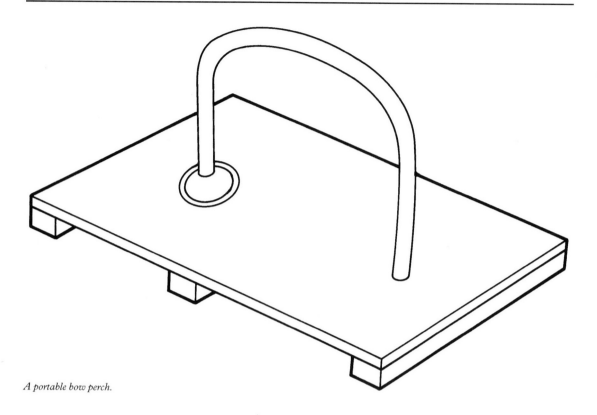

A portable bow perch.

perches are fitted with two metal spikes instead of weights, which are driven into the weathering lawn to secure the perch. The static perches are my personal favourite, although obviously they rely on a suitable lawn for their use. Once driven home they are secure, and the falconer can leave his bird safe in the knowledge that she is securely tethered – and also less capable of breaking valuable flight feathers when bating because of the soft lawn underwing.

If your bird is a bater (which all hawks and buzzards are to some extent), always think about where you weather her; a harsh weathering surface can cause untold damage to feathers and even bones. Some sort of grip should be placed on the perch so the bird's feet have something to grab. Astroturf (synthetic grass often used on sports pitches) is a popular favourite, as is leather padding. This must, of course, be weatherproof. Suitable material underfoot for your bird can also help prevent the dreaded Bumblefoot (see Chapter 4).

Blocks can be easily fashioned in their simplest form by finding a suitable log and driving a metal spike into it for securing to the weathering lawn. A

metal ring will also need to be attached on to which to tie the leash.

Generally speaking, falcons do not bate as much or as powerfully as buzzards and hawks, so you need not worry as much about the solidity of their seating (although it should still be secure).

Argument has raged over what sort of material should be used to cover the block. Some say simple stone – after all, that is what your falcon would likely be sitting on in the wild. My own feeling is that this is too cold a material. In the wild, rocks and stones would also be cold, but the wild bird has the choice to move; circulation is also probably more effective in a wild bird than in a tethered one, and anything that may cause potential problems in your bird's feet should be cast aside. Others say cork is an excellent topping off material. Most simply opt for a simple wood finish, while others go for some sort of synthetic material such as astroturf.

The main thing is to ensure that your bird is suitably protected from the elements and comfortable at all times. She is going to spend long periods on her block, so any weakness in it is going to

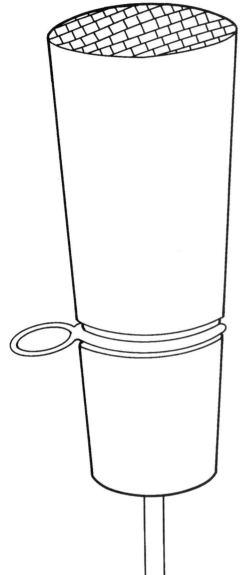

eventually find a way through, which may result in injury or infection. If you are at all concerned, try another material. With a little experience, you will easily be able to tell if your bird looks uncomfortable.

SECURING FURNITURE

Also on your furniture list are the instruments that are actually going to secure your hawk when she is not flying. In falconry this is done by means of leather strips attached to her legs, which are in turn attached to a strong leash which is ultimately tied to her block/perch.

JESS

The leather strips are called jesses.

Old-fashioned jesses were an all-in-one affair, however these have virtually been replaced by a far quicker method entailing a leather anklet made to fit your bird's leg, with a brass eyelet at the back.

Jesses can simply be threaded through the eyelet, stopping by means of a simple knot at the end, thick enough so it does not pass through the eyelet. They can be removed quickly and easily, and although the old-fashioned type may be useful in an emergency, the newer variety (known as Aylmeri after the late Guy Aylmer who first introduced their use) have completely replaced them in modern falconry.

Again, only the best leather should be used for anklets and jesses, as they are the only things stopping your bird disappearing into the blue. I would recommend kangaroo leather. It is relatively expensive, but is incredibly strong, and a decent set

A block.

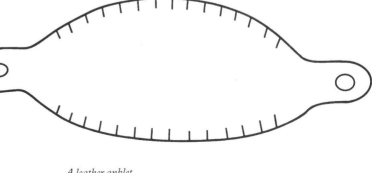

A leather anklet.

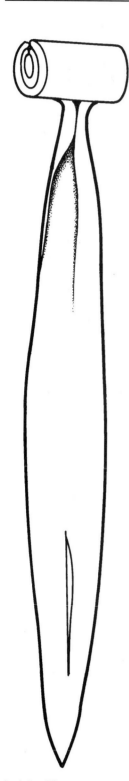

Different sizes and types of traditional jess.

An Aylmeri Jess.

Astroturf, available in sheets used for doormats!

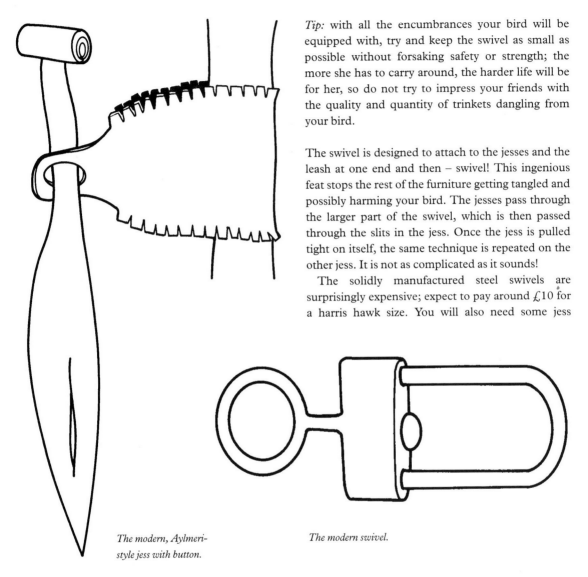

Tip: with all the encumbrances your bird will be equipped with, try and keep the swivel as small as possible without forsaking safety or strength; the more she has to carry around, the harder life will be for her, so do not try to impress your friends with the quality and quantity of trinkets dangling from your bird.

The swivel is designed to attach to the jesses and the leash at one end and then – swivel! This ingenious feat stops the rest of the furniture getting tangled and possibly harming your bird. The jesses pass through the larger part of the swivel, which is then passed through the slits in the jess. Once the jess is pulled tight on itself, the same technique is repeated on the other jess. It is not as complicated as it sounds!

The solidly manufactured steel swivels are surprisingly expensive; expect to pay around £10 for a harris hawk size. You will also need some jess

The modern, Aylmeri-style jess with button.

The modern swivel.

of jesses cut from quality kangaroo should last all season (and probably longer, although it makes sense to change them, just to be on the safe side).

SWIVEL

Along from your jesses is a swivel.

These are simple affairs, but need to be good quality, therefore my advice is to buy these in. They come in a range of sizes, from tiny ones to those large enough to take the oomph out of a determined eagle, so it is best to discuss your requirements with your chosen dealer.

grease to keep your leather supple and prolong its useful life. This can be made by mixing ordinary candle wax and paraffin, or bought in from a dealer for a few pounds. Treat all leather equipment every couple of weeks or so to keep them going and to waterproof them.

BELLS AND BEWIT

Leather strips are also needed to attach a bell to the bird's leg; this is called a bewit. Discordant bells should be used in pairs, so the ring is louder and carries a greater distance.

There are many sizes of swivel available.

The other bell is traditionally mounted onto the bird's tail (especially on shortwings, who have a habit of tail-waggling every time they hop onto a new branch). The bell is attached to a thin strip of leather, which is passed through two holes punched in a guitar plectrum and then onto the two deck (centre) tail feathers of the hawk. This is then either glued safely in position or sewn on using wax thread and a curved needle. In this way the bell sits flush against the feathers and is able to ring clearly at the slightest movement. This is a great help in finding a hawk in deep cover, or following a freshly made kill when the bird is instinctively still so as not to alert any other predators to the fact there is food around.

LEASH

The final item on the checklist from bird to your glove is the leash. This is used to attach the swivel to your glove, or indeed your fist. These days, nearly everyone uses round Terylene material for leashes, the type used in sailing for rigging, for example. It is immensely strong, pliable and easily washable. In olden days, leashes were also made of flat leather, but take my advice and go for the easier option.

The end of the leash passes through the small ring of your swivel and is stopped passing straight through by a knot at the other end. This is usually tied then gingerly burnt to seal the knot. A leather washer is placed between knot and swivel and you have a very strong leash that should be able to handle most sizes of bird.

It is recommended that your leash be around 4ft long. When tying your bird it is important not to give them too long a leash; if they bate and get a bit of speed up, the subsequent repeated jarring of joints and muscles can cause problems and injuries. You will need two leashes, one to use while the other is being washed (it is quite safe to throw your leashes in

A bell.

A bell attached to a guitar plectrum, ready to be tail-mounted.

the washing machine), and it is best to go for dull colours like dark green or black to avoid enticing your hawk to picking at it. This can occur, indeed some birds do their best to emulate Harry Houdini and become experts at unpicking your falconers' knot.

Special measures are needed to combat this (more knots), but generally speaking it is best to prevent your bird even getting interested in picking at her furniture. Most birds usually forget about it soon enough.

You can tie your leash to the metal ring attached to your glove as you hold her to stop her bating off, but

I prefer the traditional method of carrying your bird. At this stage, it seems appropriate to add a warning: most falconers lose a bird at some stage, whether it be for a few minutes or permanently. It goes with the territory and no-one will think any the less of you if you should have such an unfortunate experience. However, there is a sacred rule. Never, ever, should a hawk get away while still trailing her furniture. It would be more humane to shoot her. Leash, swivel or jesses will inevitably get tangled in a tree and the more she thrashes about, the more your pride and joy will tangle herself. Unless you are very, very lucky, she will die a long, lingering and awful death

Jesses, swivel and leash combine to keep your bird safely tethered.

Most birds pick at their equipment, but generally give it up after a time.

Employing Safety A: thread the leash through the swivel and double it ...

... lock the leash around your little finger...

... and make a loose, tidy loop.

hanging upside down from some lofty branch.

This can be prevented by single-minded dedication to the two types of safety position you should use while handling your bird. They are as follows:

(1) The bird is sitting on your fist, you have just untied her from her perch and you are holding the leash in your other hand. Take hold of the knot at the end of the leash and pull it until your leash is doubled. Both pieces of leash are then locked tightly around your little finger. The 'leftovers' go between

the second and third fingers (some use the first and second) and are made into a loose, tidy loop.

This is neat, unobtrusive and can be undone in seconds. But most importantly, it is impossible for your bird to escape. She can bate to her heart's content if she insists, but will simply have to climb back onto your fist. This is what I call Safety A.

(2) Safety B comes into play when you are taking off the bird's furniture for flying, or picking her up and putting her into her night quarters. Obviously, there will be no leash involved here. As soon as she is on

Employing Safety B: with the jesses and swivel at the back of the hand, they cannot be pulled through easily.

the fist, both jesses must be picked up and passed between the second and third fingers so that they appear at the back of the hand. If necessary, they can also be locked into the little finger for added security. When the swivel is in place, it sits on the outside of your fingers, providing a useful stop to the jesses slipping through and your bird disappearing. Simply close your fist and your bird cannot go anywhere.

If you keep your hawk in either safety position at all times she is under your direct control, you will have nothing to reproach yourself about. If, however, you fail to ensure your bird's safety and she slips away, you do not possess the self-discipline necessary to repeat the safety process *every* time you pick your bird up and should not consider taking up falconry.

CREANCE

The creance is a thin cotton line tied to a stick, and is used during the training of birds for falconry. One end of the line is passed through your bird's swivel and tied off. In this way the bird can be set on fence posts and flown over longer and longer distances during her training. Should she suddenly decide enough is enough and try to disappear, you will be able to hang on to her thanks to the creance. It trails behind the bird as she flies, and as long as you do not fly her where there are any snags or long grass, it should cause her no concern.

Typically, a creance can be unwound to lengths of around 50yd before it runs out. Once your bird is coming rapidly to you over this distance, you are ready to try her free. A creance can be a handy thing to have with you at all times, and you cannot properly train your bird without one. I advise you not to try and make your own; the line needs to be thin, lightweight and strong and you need to know you can rely on it. Invest in one from a quality furniture maker. You can pick them up for around £10.

A creance.

LURE

If you intend to fly longwings, you will also need a lure. This is used to call in your falcon, and also to exercise her before flying her at live quarry. It is supposed to represent the flying quarry your falcon would normally be hunting. As well as being a

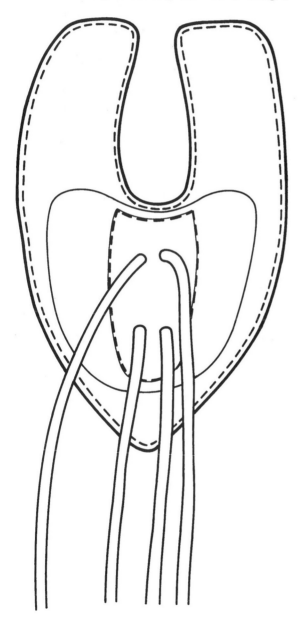

A lure.

sturdily constructed piece of falconry furniture, there is a knack to using a lure, one that I have to admit I struggle with. You may have seen them at country fairs or shows. Experienced falconers make their use look deceptively easy as the falcon swoops in for a pass, but believe me, there is a real skill to good lure work.

The lure can consist of a horseshoe piece of leather filled with stuffing and attached to a long line, or more simply a pair of dried rook's wings. The flapping of the wings attracts the attention of the falcon, who stoops in to try and grab the lure which is suitably garnished with meat. The falconer leads her on several passes, just swinging the lure out of her reach at the last second, before he finally lets her catch it and take her reward. Falcons can put on real muscle and speed after being trained to the lure and it gives them a chance to practise a little aerobatics before being pitched at fit, live quarry.

Patterns for leather lures are available for copying, but they can also be bought ready to use from furniture makers. Expect to pay £15–20.

DUMMY BUNNY

If your preference is for short- and broadwings, you will need a dummy bunny so they are able to practise their technique. This is even simpler than the lure and can definitely be cobbled together at home. All that is needed is something of roughly rabbit size and colour (a white scut is very useful as it shows the bird what a running rabbit would really look like) which can be attached to a creance and dragged out of bushes, grass, and so on, to get your bird used to expecting chances to grab prey. My dummy bunny (affectionately known as Bernard) is, in fact, a toy rabbit. He is the right colour, has a nice white fluffy tail and has been chased up and down miles of hedgerow! Dummy bunnies can also be bought in for around £20.

HAWKING KNIFE

A knife is another essential item. This is necessary for all sorts of useful tasks while out in the field

A falcon stooping to the lure. Note the radio microphone being used to give a running commentary while conducting the complicated task of successful lure-swinging.

Bernard the dummy bunny!

Sheath knife.

(cutting twine or trimming well-used paths through brambles), but it is mainly used for dispatching quarry quickly should your bird fail to do so.

Contrary to the opinion of some falconers, I prefer a single blade sheath knife rather than the lockable blade type. As a falconer is desired to carry out most tasks with just one hand, it seems odd to relax the rules when it comes to a knife; you could well need to use your knife when your bird is on your fist, and just try opening a lock knife with one hand. A solid blade, however, when attached by its sheath to your belt, can swiftly be retrieved and brought into play. It is also less likely to be lost than lock knives, which you may well stuff in a pocket in a moment of excitement and then lose the next time you clamber over a stile. As with all knives, the blade should be kept scrupulously sharp and should have a good point.

Tip: avoid 10in 'commando'-style knives. Apart from making you look like a complete idiot when wearing it on your belt, it will be cumbersome and weighty in the field. It also does not do to wander around advertising the fact that you are armed. It could alarm anyone not necessarily fully furnished with the intricacies of the sport.

HAWKING BAG

A hawking bag is very useful, if not absolutely essential. You will need something in which to keep pieces of meat (usually referred to as pick-up pieces) which are used to call your bird into the fist, or to get her attention when she has killed. Also, all things being well, your charge will eventually catch something. Whether you intend to keep it for

A useful hawking bag, originally intended for fishermen.

The necessary field kit: hawking bag, creance, binoculars, knife, hawking glove, whistle on lanyard, spare jesses and a first aid kit.

additional hawk food or as a tasty treat for your own pot, you will need somewhere to stash it (your bird will not tactfully leave its catch if asked, like a dog. If you continue to walk on, swinging a recently caught rabbit beside you, you will soon find a bird of prey attached as well. Not until your bird thinks the food has disappeared will it start looking elsewhere once more).

The hawking bag can be made from canvas and custom-constructed to your own requirements; mine is actually a fishing bag, of the type used by trout anglers. It has a number of useful-sized pockets and, best of all, a detachable inner plastic lining. This is indispensable for it serves well for carrying caught quarry and can later be rinsed clean under the tap.

Traditional hawking bags can be expensive to buy

(up to £50), and vary from those attached to your belt to those you can sling over a shoulder via a strap. Mine is of the latter type, and these fishing-style bags can be bought at a significantly cheaper price than the 'proper' hawking bags. My advice would be to take a look at both sorts and make your own mind up.

HAWKING ATTIRE

Some mention should be made here of hawking attire. Do not be dictated to by anyone; you are, of course, perfectly entitled to wear whatever you like. It obviously pays to wear 'country'-style clothing, however, as you will find yourself out and about in some very cold, wet, muddy, or even thorny conditions and terrain, and suitable attire is essential to protect you and ensure you can concentrate on enjoying your hawking.

For both warmth and its thornproof qualities, I have yet to come across anything to rival good old-fashioned moleskin (and to please the traditionalists, this is quite suitable hawking get-up!). It is incredibly comfortable, warm and cosy, and is capable of protecting you from many sharp prods and scrapes. It also has pretty effective waterproofing. On the downside, 'moles' are expensive – around £30 for a pair of trousers in the UK, and you can pay considerably more.

A decent pair of wellington boots is essential, and should probably be higher up this list. If you can

Ready for the fields! If you intend to use a working dog you will need to spend time getting the bird used to her new companion.

afford them (expect to pay around £50 for a pair), splash out on a really good pair – you will never regret it. They are worth their weight in gold in the field. They are supple, lovely and warm, and, best of all, cling to your calves unlike normal 'off the peg' wellies. The latter are also perfectly adequate to do the job in question, which is keep your feet dry, but they tend to flap around at the tops of your calves, and after you have spent a few minutes in long grass, brambles and blackthorn (which is inevitable if you are a falconer) you will find your wellies full of twigs, burrs and other uncomfortable nuisances. You will have to empty them every few minutes and this becomes a real pain (I speak from experience, yet again).

A shirt and decent sweater are always a necessity (since we do our hawking in the winter) and more often than not a quality coat is also needed. Choose whatever makes you feel comfortable and is likely to be warm, but remember that you may have to do a lot of walking (or occasionally running!) and so you should be able to move freely; you also do not want to overheat. Bear in mind that your colours should be muted unless you want to stick out like a sore thumb. I have opted for a tweed-style jacket, which has proved to be considerably warmer than a waxed jacket. Tweed is also suitably rainproof and has been used by generations of gamekeepers as their traditional everyday garb. It is, however, perhaps something to wait until Christmas for; a half-decent tweed is unlikely to cost you much less than £100, although bargains can be picked up at game fairs, for example.

Fingerless gloves can be helpful in really bad weather, but I tend not to bother. You will need only

When calling your bird in from a distance, a quality whistle is a God-send.

Time spent scanning with binoculars is never wasted, and they will come in very handy when your bird disappears in hot pursuit of quarry!

one because you have a gauntlet on the other hand.

And finally, one of the most important aspects must be The Silly Hat! Most of your body heat is lost through the top of your head, so a good hat is essential to keep warm on those chilly winter mornings. I have opted for the traditional tweed flat cap style, which, while being perfect for the job, does tend to make one look like a chimney urchin, hence 'The Silly Hat'. No-one should be without one; they are waterproof, warm, and to be honest, they really do look the part!

WHISTLE

A whistle is a useful addition to the armoury. I use a staghorn whistle, which has a piercing tone that carries for a long way, and which is nice to look at, although virtually any sort of whistle will do as long as the sound carries. I rarely use mine, being happy to rely on my own vocal whistle, but it is a comfort to know I can give a really good, ear-piercing blast if needs be.

Tip: make sure your whistle is on a lanyard round your neck and not tucked in a pocket, otherwise you will inevitably lose it, no matter how careful you are.

BINOCULARS

Not only is a pair of binoculars essential for reconnaissance missions on your hawking terrain, they also come in remarkably handy when your bird is 'missing in action'. Consider investing in a lightweight pair that can be clipped to your belt and forgotten about until they are needed, although I actually opted for a heavier, chunkier pair for the stability they offer. A good pair retails at £100 or less these days.

There are umpteen other gadgets and encumbrances that you will collect over time: a flask for those cold days; a small camera to capture some of those falconry 'moments'; a sandwich box for day-long trips – the list is endless.

4 ACCOMMODATION AND DAILY MAINTENANCE

The biggest concern in falconry is, of course, the well-being of your charge. She must be warm, dry, clean and content at all times – as far as is humanly possible – and it will take some time to figure out how best to achieve this.

NIGHT QUARTERS (NQ)

This is basically a glorified box, which has always been known as 'night quarters'. The name speaks for itself; when the falconer brings in his bird for the night, it provides a warm, safe haven where she can sleep unmolested and out of the way of the worst of winter's ignominies. The NQ is also used in times of emergency, such as when the bird is sick or injured and needs warmth, darkness and solitude.

Again, as with so much falconry equipment, this can be as grand or as plain as you like, as long as it serves the purpose. The design must be big enough to comfortably house your bird as she sits on a perch. For most species 2ft by 2ft is perfectly adequate. My own NQ was designed and built by a good friend who happens to be a carpenter. It is pretty big, 2ft by 3ft, and is a hefty thing to move, but it provides an excellent resting place for Archie. His name is even stencilled on the front! The solid box has been lined with plastic so it can be easily wiped clean (do not forget this or your box will soon become stained with mutes, and will eventually start to rot. This in turn will increase the chance of illness so should be avoided at all costs). It is best fitted with a well-topped log or wide perch to spread the weight of the bird and reduce pressure on the feet. Some plain

Night quarters.
Notice the air holes
and a log to provide
comfortable perching.

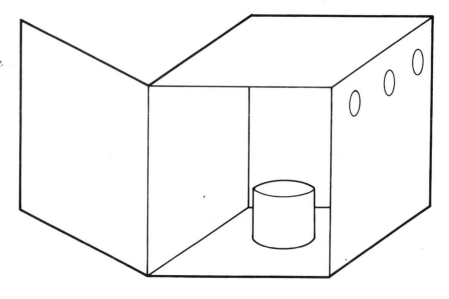

plastic bubble wrap tacked to the door immediately in front of the perch can be useful. This is because some birds – Archie included – have a tendency to leap off the perch and jump at the door when they think it is time for them to be let out. The bubble wrap stops them injuring their wings or ceres on the hard surface.

Every night, I tack newspaper to the back and floor of the box (usually double thickness) which collects the worst of the overnight mutes. The paper can simply be taken out, the box wiped clean, and new paper installed each night. It is quick and easy and saves a lot of time.

Tip: when constructing your bird's masterpiece, do not overlook the most obvious and important thing: breathing holes. Three decent-sized holes on either side of the box near the top where they cannot be obstructed should suffice.

Ensure your box is smooth and clean internally; the last thing you want is your bird to suffer an injury thanks to a protruding nail or splinter. A latch or bolt on the door is also a sensible precaution. Always make sure your bird's furniture is removed before you put her away; if jesses and a swivel are still attached, this could create all sorts of problems, particularly if you prefer a block rather than a perch in your NQ. Your bird could easily straddle the block, becoming trapped by the jesses. It is very easy to break tail feathers in this way.

If your NQ is of a sensible size (and not the monstrous thing I demanded!) it can also be used as a travelling box in your car, so your bird can travel in safety and comfort, without too much undue stress.

FALCONRY ROOM/MEWS

If at all possible, it is advisable to convert a small shed or outbuilding into your falconry room, or 'mews' to use the old-fashioned term. In this way, you can collect all your equipment in one place and things can be arranged to suit your own taste.

A food larder, with gauze fitted to allow safe defrosting away from flies.

Ideally, your NQ can stand in one corner, somewhere warm and out of the way, and the rest of the room can be dedicated to your remaining gear. Some falconers have fabulous custom-built mews, but I feel fortunate to have the use of our old shed (which also houses the washing machine, freezer, gardening tools and anything else deemed unfit to go in the house). In your mews, you will need a box in which to keep thawing or fresh hawk food (a small box fitted with a gauze top is ideal to let air circulate and prevent inquisitive flies getting in). It is best to add a small latch to this so nothing can get at your bird's food before it does. I hasten to add that I, of course, had nothing to do with the construction of my hawk food box; again it was kindly donated by a friend and fellow falconer.

Some shelves or a cabinet would be useful in your mews, in which to keep medical equipment. More shelves or draws will be necessary to house your basic leatherwork kit, while a worktop is also handy as somewhere to place your scales, and finally a few hooks should be dotted about for leashes, hawking bags, swivels and jesses.

Tip: hang your glove up out of the way when it is not in use. Many have been damaged irreparably by hungry mice drawn by the exotic smell of a falconry glove!

If you are in the enviable position of being able to construct your own mews from scratch, the sky is really the limit. Ideally, you would want a room lined with tiles and sloping towards an inbuilt drain so that cleaning is simple. Any windows should have bars fitted across so they can be opened without fear of your bird escaping (make sure the bars are vertically placed so your hawk cannot grab onto them, and ensure they are placed close enough together so she cannot squeeze through. You would be surprised!).

The 'inner mews' can be fitted with a suitable perch and front screen perhaps, with an outer room of a decent size. Make sure the door between the two opens inward to prevent mad dashes for freedom (or at least make them easier to cope with). The outer mews can be as luxurious as you like, depending on whether or not you plan to stay out there for any length of time. A table, chair, set of drawers,

blackboard for daily weights, and so on, are all most useful. Some sort of worksurface for jess-making and other odd jobs would be of benefit. And if you have the time and inclination, you could also make up some wall cupboards for medicines, cleaning equipment and the countless other odds and ends you will pick up along the way. Hooks and shelves for tools, bells, gloves and the like are essential.

A freezer is another necessity. You will need it to store supplies of hawk food. It is highly unlikely that you will be able to keep up a constant supply of fresh meat; as you are no doubt thinking, the expense just keeps adding up! And I'm afraid there's more to come.

THE WEATHERING LAWN

'Blocking out' is the term used to describe the action of setting out a falcon's block on the weathering lawn, but is equally adept for describing the same procedure for the bow perch of the short or broadwing. Your bird is blocked onto the weathering lawn in all but the worst weather and can enjoy the obvious benefits of fresh air, sunshine, the odd drizzle, and an unrestricted view.

The weathering lawn is the most preferable of all accommodation, but unfortunately one of the most impractical.

There are precious few among us able to be on hand all day every day, within spitting distance of our weathering lawn, should the heavens open or some similar disaster befall your bird. It is simply not good enough to check the weather forecast and hope it will not rain too heavily on your unprotected bird while you go off to work.

The elements are not all you have to worry about. Predators such as cats or foxes may become too inquisitive. And perhaps more of a worry are two-legged intruders. Birds of prey do have some significant monetary value, and apart from that, people are naturally nosy. There have been some disastrous tales of birds injured or killed by intruders who stumbled across them.

So, if you have to go elsewhere at some stage during your day, then you will need to provide some sort of protection and housing for your charge. Once

Blocking out in the shade of a tree is fine while you are in the vicinity, but careful thought will have to be given to the care of your bird when you are away.

again, this can be as simple or as elaborate as you like, as long as it is big enough to house a block/bow perch. In its simplest form, your weathering can be a three-sided affair, just big enough to comfortably house your bird and with a sloping roof to keep off the worst of the weather. A front fenced panel can be added or removed as and when it is needed, and secured with a padlock to give you some peace of mind when you leave your bird untended. If at all possible, your weathering should be sited to offer a little sun in the morning, and shelter from the worst heat in the afternoon. Cover from the prevailing wind is also needed to prevent your bird's stamina being gradually worn down.

If you have the space you can really go to town and erect a first-class shelter that allows your bird some freedom of movement, the chance to get some sun, air and rain if she wants, and the opportunity to get under cover if things become too rough.

These shelters can be fitted with dead tree limbs, rocks, inbuilt baths, perches, ledges, and so on, to make your bird really feel at home. As well as having some freedom of movement, your hawk will also have the opportunity to work her breast and wing muscles, keeping her fitter, improving circulation and generally increasing her chances of remaining in tip-top condition. These shelters are, in my opinion, the best possible option.

A young or inexperienced bird may 'crash around' in these pens, unaware of the fencing, and may damage themselves in the process, so it is best to allow them plenty of time tethered to the bow perch inside before they are allowed free. My bird spent virtually all of his first season tethered in his shelter after crashing into the front wire mesh. He badly bruised his cere, which in turn kept getting knocked while flying, and the injury took months and months to grow out. Be warned: birds breathe through their

It's very useful to have friends who know what they are doing! Here the final touches are being made to an ideal hawk shelter.

nasal passages and any cere damage can be disastrous, resulting in them being unable to fly or worse. I was lucky to catch the injury before too much damage was done, but again falconry taught me a harsh lesson. It has a nasty habit of punishing shortcomings very severely. If your bird shows the slightest tendency to crash into the front mesh, and you are concerned, get some thin gardening netting and stretch it tight over the inside of the wire. This should prevent any serious damage until your hawk calms down somewhat.

Your shelter can be constructed of any sort of material, indeed a good solid brick foundation would be hard to beat. That is not very practical for most of us, however, so you will find the majority of shelters are built from wood. Fencing panels are fine if your weathering ground is not too exposed to wind. The roof will need to be felted, and can even be fitted with a length of guttering to keep rainfall away, if you choose. The type of wire mesh you use is very important. It must be thick gauge and coated in

plastic. Under no circumstances allow your bird anywhere near bare wire. It will cut her to ribbons. Black-coated wire is the best, as you can see through it more easily into the weathering. Before you construct your bird's luxury daytime accommodation, remember to treat it well with varnish. This should keep it in good condition for several years at least.

The base of the weathering should be covered with plain chicken wire to prevent any wild animal burying up into it, then covered with a generous thickness of pea shingle. Debate has raged about what should be used to cover the base of weatherings; suggestions include sand and sawdust. To my mind, good old-fashioned gravel is hard to beat. Yes, it may be a little hard, but as long as you go for the small-size stones, it should not cause any damage to your bird as she bates. It is also relatively easily cleaned. Soiled areas can be removed, sprayed with disinfectant and raked over. I do not like the idea of sand, as once wet it would get everywhere and stick to the bird. Sawdust or wood chippings should also be avoided. Fungal disease and dampness can quickly take a hold in these conditions and it will only be a matter of time before your bird picks up a nasty infection, quite possibly respiratory. This is obviously to be avoided at all costs.

A good old dead limb with some perching branches is ideal furniture for your hawk's apartment.

Tip: do not put perches, logs, branches or anything else in your shelter until your bird is ready to go in untethered. She will simply bate at them all day long, trying to get to them, and will wear herself out.

Once free inside, though, she will love hopping between her perches, checking out the vantage points and will no doubt soon discover a favourite. Just make sure the branches have no sharp protrusions and are not mouldy. If at all possible, try and place your perches where mutes will not soil the sides of your shelter.

A cut length of log can also be placed inside, provided it is well dried. It can be utilized as a table top, preventing food being grubbed around on the floor. Alternatively, a rock or boulder can be put in place. This will help keep down your bird's talons, stopping them growing. You may find she also uses it for feaking (stropping her beak clean). This in turn will keep beak growth in check.

Ledges are also popular, again as food tables, and a swinging perch is a real winner. Attach it to the roof struts (ensuring there is plenty of head room so your bird can jump onto it). If you site it at the front of your weathering, she will be able to sit there swaying gently in the breeze while soaking up the warming rays of the early morning sun!

A bird bath is another essential item in your weathering. These can be bought in but are pretty expensive. Alternatively, an upturned dustbin lid can be used, or decent sized plastic containers can sometimes be found at garden centres. Not all birds like baths; many only take them occasionally, and some never at all, but all should be given the opportunity. It keeps feathers in pristine condition, reduces the chance of parasites and encourages preening. If my bird does not have the chance of a bath for some time, he simply disappears on his own the next time we go flying and takes one himself. Be warned: a wet bird flies poorly.

A swing perch – of suitable circumference and covered properly – provides excellent support for your hawk.

Archie in his juvenile year; note the cere bruising caused by bating into his wire mesh.

If you find, like I did, that you cannot position your weathering ideally to both catch the sun and provide a shelter from the wind, all is not lost.

Although my shelter provided an ample windbreak, because of the angle of the sun it never received any warming rays directly.

This was obviously not ideal, so I decided to take a couple of feet off the roof, meshing over the top so that Archie could benefit from a bit of sun, at least in part of his shelter. I strung up his swinging perch under this open space so he could sit there in whatever weather he liked. He rarely sits anywhere else now.

Tip: if you decide to amend your shelter in a similar way, do not forget to refelt round the edge to ensure no water gets in. Also make sure you have some suitable weld mesh to cover the overhead gap. Netting will do as long as it is taut enough to avoid your bird getting in a tangle.

The front door should be of a reasonable height and width so you can come and go without too much trouble. In fact, the bigger you can make your

Siting of your shelter is important. There must be shade, protection from the worst of the wind and rain, and plenty for your hawk to see.

Refilling the water bath should be a frequent task.

Leaving the front part of your shelter uncovered gives your bird more sun and the chance of a shower.

shelter, the better for your hawk. The most practical size, however, is around 6ft by 6ft. This is plenty big enough for birds up to reasonable size and will offer them a degree of freedom that many unfortunately never get. Put a nice handle on your door to avoid having to grasp and yank the mesh, therefore pulling it out of shape, and invest in a decent padlock or locking latch; although nothing is going to deter the most dedicated of thieves, you should aim for as much security as possible.

The most important thing is not to do half a job on your aviary. If you are anything like me, do not attempt to construct it yourself. It will only get blown over in the first breeze. Instead, pay for a sturdy and reliable shelter that is going to keep your bird safe and warm in the worst weather.

DAILY ROUTINE AND MAINTENANCE

A good falconer should handle his bird at least twice a day during the flying season, getting her out of her night quarters and putting her into her shelter and vice versa at the end of the day. The more time spent with any bird, the better. The more they are handled and manned, the better behaved they will become.

These two handling periods should also give the experienced falconer enough time to check over the condition of his bird. Does anything look untoward? Is she quiet, fluffed up and lethargic, or screaming, leaping about and breathing heavily? Any abnormalities should be picked up simply by checking over these and other points mentally as you go through the drill of attaching jesses, swivel and leash. As with most health matters in any species, early detection and treatment saves lives.

Every day, several procedures should be followed. Equipment should be checked over quickly to ensure no sudden and unforeseen breakages occur which could result in loss or injury. Is the leather on your jesses still strong and sturdy? A good tug will suffice; look for any signs of tearing or thinning, especially around the button and the slit for the swivel. Similarly, are the anklets still in good shape and supple enough not to cause discomfort? Checks on the leash should be made periodically, again especially around the button, and although decent swivels should last forever, they should be given the once over occasionally, too.

Once your hawk has been removed from her night quarters, weighed in for the day and placed in her shelter, you then have to decide when to feed her. This, of course, depends on when or whether you intend to fly her later on. Feeding times should really be kept to some sort of routine. If you feed at the same time every day, you can be safe in the knowledge that your bird's weight is true as there will be no food left in the stomach from the last feed, and she will have 'cast'.

All birds of prey regurgitate the indigestible parts of their food, such as bones, fur, feathers, and so on, in the form of a pellet. You cannot fly your bird until she has cast, so getting into a routine will ensure you know she has already cast by a certain hour. Casting usually occurs 12-18 hours after feeding.

If you can, feed your bird on the fist as much as possible. It helps to maintain a bond between you, and she will look forward to seeing you as she knows it often means a feed.

A casting.

The shape of the beak should be carefully monitored and regularly trimmed. Note the tooth on this hybrid's beak; falcons use it for dislocating the vertebrae of their prey.

The more infrequent husbandry essentials include worming your hawk every six months or so with a general-purpose wormer, and anti-mite spray should be used every once in a while to prevent feather and skin infections.

COPING

Coping is the term used to describe the act of trimming and shaping the hawk's beak.

In the wild this would occur naturally through the continuous breaking into tough prey and feaking on stones. But the falconer's bird does not often have these privileges and so needs some help. Do not undertake the task of coping without first having been shown the ropes by an expert. Just like our own toe- and fingernails, beaks have a quick and can bleed profusely if they are cut back too harshly (this also applies to *pounces*, or talons).

If the falcon is left uncoped her upper mandible will gradually grow downwards into a ridiculous curve and will not sit flush with the lower one. In extreme cases, the bird finds it increasingly difficult to eat unaided. Listen out for a small clicking noise if you are unsure whether or not your bird needs coping. This noise is often heard when friction begins between the two mandibles. Ideally, coping should be carried out before this stage is reached, however.

Alternatively, refer to pictures and drawings of hawks and falcons to see how the beak should look. Once the beak has been sufficiently taken back with a pair of clippers (the sort you would use on a dog's claws are eminently suitable), it must be carefully shaped once more. Many falconers have different methods of doing this, using a variety of rounded, flat and triangular graded files to give the beak that graceful curve. One friend even uses an expensive electric manicure set! A selection of nail files is usually enough to carry out the task competently. Any cracks in the beak must be filed out, and the cut edge should be softened and rounded to suit the rest of the curve of the beak. Simply touching and feeling along the beak can give you an excellent impression of how it should eventually end up. Once your handiwork is complete, moisten the tips of the fingers and run them over the beak to ensure no hard splinters remain.

Tip: do not get carried away! It is easy to start trimming a beak and end up taking a lot more off than you originally bargained for. Remember that little is more; it is better to leave the beak long than distress your bird by taking it back too much.

IMPING

Imping is something that all falconers hope to avoid, but eventually have to face at some time in their career. It is simply the art of replacing a lost feather, where it has been inopportunely broken or lost along the way. The loss of any feather can be quite an inconvenience to a bird, and if it is a flight feather things can become even more sinister.

A wild bird who has broken a primary, secondary or train feather is in big trouble, for each of these feathers plays a crucial role in flight and therefore in hunting. This is why birds are so fastidious about their preening. Feathers need to be kept in tip-top condition for everyday use.

Without 100 per cent flight fitness, the bird stands less chance against its chosen quarry and suddenly its chances of survival start to nosedive. Thankfully for the falconer's bird, these occasional breakages can be nothing more than a nuisance if dealt with efficiently.

Once a feather breaks, the first thing to ascertain is where the break has occurred. Sometimes, if the whole feather has come free, it is possible to reinsert so that it continues to provide sterling service. However, more often than not this is not the case and the feather breaks further up the quill.

This is where 'imping' comes in. A small peg is created (usually a piece of gardening cane or similar) and trimmed so that it fits snugly into the broken-off quill. The other end is similarly trimmed to ensure it fits into the end of the quill still in the bird (these two ends may also need trimming to achieve a suitable fit). When the correct fit is ascertained, the two ends of quill are glued onto the peg, which acts as a splint. Although that feather will not grow back, the peg should be sufficiently strong to last until the next moult and allow the hawk to manoeuvre its feather without feeling the slightest difference.

Sometimes it is not possible to rescue a feather if it is bashed beyond repair or broken too close to the end. Then another feather can be imped in its place.

Keep your collected moult feathers in a sealed container.

However, this *must* be as close a match as possible for the sake of the bird's flight powers as well as her looks. Once I was appalled to see a snowy owl feather imped onto the train-tail of a harris hawk. The snowy's feather served no useful purpose to the hawk, and, being bright white, merely served to draw unwanted attention to the bird.

The moult will be discussed in due course, but suffice to say every year your hawk will shed all its feathers over an extended period. Important flight feathers should therefore be kept from last year's moult in case they are needed the following season. Wherever possible, it makes sense to replace a right-hand primary with a right-hand primary, and so on. This is not always possible though, so go for the nearest available match. The feathers are best kept in a sealed container, away from sunlight, dust and excessive heat. Preservation in a freezer has also been mooted as a good way of keeping them in pristine condition. Feathers just placed in a pot on your worktop will soon get dusty, out of shape and dirty.

Again, do not attempt to imp your hawk until someone with experience has shown you how.

Tip: be wary of glue! Any number of accidents can befall you while you are imping, so be careful not to

Talons, or pounces, should be kept short enough so that the bird can comfortably stand flat-footed.

Keeping your bird in mint flying condition and prime health is your main responsibility. This is largely achieved through good accommodation and provision of the right nutrients.

glue your fingers to the splint, the bird, the table, and so on. Also, be extremely careful not to get any on adjoining feathers. If in doubt – ask for help.

HAWK FOOD

Your bird needs fresh meat daily. She is not a vegetarian and requires a balanced diet, which means a variety of animals. If the thought makes you squeamish, falconry is not for you.

You must start by insisting on a golden rule: know exactly where the meat you feed your bird comes from and how it met its end. It is tempting to pick up a freshly killed pheasant carcass on the road because hawks will love it. But why is it there? Was it hit by a

car because it was sick/injured and slow? Had it been shot? A single lead pellet is enough to kill your bird. Even if I hit a rabbit myself in the car, I do not pick it up. There is no way of telling if it is clean.

When your bird eventually kills, it is the done thing to let her feed up a little on it. This is fine, as long as she gets her reward in fresh meat bought in from a reliable source, as you know it is uncontaminated. A good mixture should ensure your bird is getting all the nutrients she requires.

Tip: do not forget to defrost hawk food overnight. On several occasions I have fed my bird and forgotten to dig into the freezer for more food to defrost. Now I have a big sign on the mews door reminding me to **DEFROST HAWK FOOD!**

Some falconers also put supplements in their hawk's food, but this should be unnecessary if your bird is getting a good mix of foods.

Most birds of prey in captivity survive on a diet consisting largely of day-old cockerels (DOC). These are humanely killed in their thousands at poultry farms, and large quantities can be bought relatively cheaply, each individual chick blast-frozen. DOC is a pretty convenient food stuff which offers a decent meal, but should not be fed exclusively as it does lack certain nutritional qualities. A mixed diet will ensure a more healthy bird. The yolk sacs of DOCs have been said to possess too much cholesterol, and it has been suggested that they should be removed. No concrete evidence has ever been provided to back this statement up, so common sense should prevail. By all means feed complete DOCs, but perhaps not all the time; on several days of the week, remove the yolk sacs. Yolk sacs also make a terrible mess when you are feeding on the fist, so remember to remove them first.

Rats and mice make superb hawk food, and birds generally love them, although one or two display a strange dislike to rodents. To be on the safe side, many falconers gut rats before feeding them to the hawk, and cut off their tails and feet because of their sharp little claws. Gutting is a grim task with a rat due to the rather nasty smell, but seems a sensible precaution. Many birds seem to leave the intestines anyway. Cutting off the feet also prevents any problems with choking, and large rat tails are a lot of gristle for a bird of prey to digest. Again, rats and mice can be bought in at a few pence each. Big rats are generally too much for a hawk during the flying season, but can be chopped in half. They offer excellent roughage, as well as protein, calcium and minerals not present in such large quantities in DOCs. Whole rats are excellent food during the moult when weight is not an issue. Believe it or not, you can also buy frozen guinea pigs or hamsters, again ideal for when you are feeding your bird up during the moult. These can be fed whole.

Another popular but expensive hawk food is quail, again bought in frozen. Quail is generally regarded as wonderful hawk food; lots of protein and excellent casting material in the feathers. Birds seem to really enjoy them. They cost around 60p each, though, and you may need up to two per day so save up those pennies!

Tip: remove the wings of quail before you feed them; a peregrine belonging to a very experienced falconer friend died after getting one trapped in its intestine. Another harsh lesson learnt.

Beef is a good quality meat to feed to hawks, providing it is stripped of all fat. The traditional feed is shin of beef, which is very cheap and quite tough; good exercise for the hawk as she pulls bits off. Beef obviously gives no castings, but this is not a problem every now and then. It is full of protein and so can cause weight to be packed on quite rapidly, so use it in small quantities during the flying season. During the moult it is an excellent alternative because it can be fed on the fist, maintaining that essential working bond between the two of you.

Although water may be present in your bird's shelter, you are unlikely to see her drink from it. Birds of prey very rarely drink water; they take the moisture their body needs from meat. Occasionally they will drink ('bowse' is the proper falconry term, from which the word 'booze' is thought to have derived), but usually only when they are feeling unwell, or when it is especially hot.

HAWK-CAUGHT FOOD

While some of the quarry your bird will catch will be eminently suitable for food, some will obviously not.

In general, I do not like the idea of my bird eating intestines and vital organs (aside from liver, which is packed with minerals), so these are assiduously removed. Only feed something you feel sure about; if you are worried about anything, play safe and remove the offending item or do not feed it at all.

• Rabbit is an excellent hawk food, and can only serve to reinforce in your hawk's mind that it is good to catch rabbits. The quality of the meat is excellent, does not cause the hawk to put on too much weight, and provides good casting material in the fur. It is worth keeping a rabbit or two in the freezer, for they are also excellent feeding during the moult, when a good piece can be given to your hawk which will be picked over all day.

• Hare is similar, although apparently a little richer than rabbit. It also tends to find its way into the falconer's pot rather than the unfortunate hawk's crop.

• Squirrel is a tough meat and therefore has some benefit in keeping a hawk gainfully occupied as she works to pull off meat. Birds seem to love it.

• Waterfowl is by its nature a greasy meat and therefore very rich. It should only be fed very occasionally in small quantities.

• Game birds are superb hawk food, providing high-quality nutrition coupled with good roughage in the form of feathers. Again, more often than not these birds end up in the kitchen rather than the mews, but a good game hawk should be rewarded occasionally with a cropful.

• Corvids (crows, rooks, magpies, and so on) seem to have a bitter flesh, which many birds of prey dislike. If your bird will take it, though, it does seem to be fairly nutritious.

• It is best not to feed pigeon to your hawk. Most wild pigeons carry a disease known as 'frounce', which shows itself via white lesions in the mouth and throat, and is easily communicated to your bird. Take no risks and avoid it altogether.

Beginners would do well to keep a diary of their early exploits, so they can see a pattern emerge which should correlate flying performance with weight, food, fitness, and so on.

HEALTHCARE

There are a number of excellent books and papers on bird-of-prey health and medicine by falconers and veterinary surgeons far better qualified than myself. I will, however, attempt to give a general overview of raptor healthcare and the illnesses and infections the falconer is most likely to come up against.

It is essential to find a good vet before you even take possession of your bird, and particularly worthwhile finding one with some expertise in avian medicine. It is also worth travelling some way to a suitable vet if one cannot be located in the immediate vicinity. You do not want to have to pay fees to a vet who does not know the difference between your bird and a budgie. At the very least, you should check that your vet would be willing to call a more experienced raptor specialist for advice if necessary.

Prevention is obviously far better than cure, and the dedicated falconer should be able to prevent many illnesses and injuries by keeping a careful eye on his charge. As well as a general everyday check-up, you should also keep an eye on the condition of your bird's mutes, as they can give a good indication as to the state of her health. Normal, healthy mutes should simply be black and white. A common condition in hawks fed solely on DOCs, however, is a brown-coloured mute. This is simply due to too rich a diet, probably caused by egg sacs. Mutes can be greenish when there is little content passing through the stomach. Bloodstained mutes could indicate parasitic infestation, and the bird should be taken to the vet if the problem is not resolved quickly.

Other crucial signs to watch for include sudden, unexplained weight loss, vomiting, fluffed up, lethargic appearance, slitted eyes and general 'out of character' behaviour.

A sick or injured hawk should be handled and disturbed as little as possible, and kept warm and well fed. Oral fluid therapy has been found to be very effective in keeping hawks alive. An electrolyte mixture can be fed directly into the crop via a tube and syringe (do not attempt this unless you are sure of what you are doing). Veterinary attention should be immediately sought.

Trauma injuries such as bites and lacerations should be treated with wound powder if bleeding is profuse, or swabbed with a saline solution or iodine for more minor injuries to prevent infection.

Bone breakages should be immobilized as soon as possible to prevent further damage. Fractures occur fairly regularly among properly hunted birds; because they are flying to hunt, they go crashing into vegetation (sometimes impenetrable), and can crack wings and legs, even toes. Broken toes are fairly common as birds strive to bind onto wildly struggling prey.

A pet carrier with suitable flooring is a useful way to transport a sick or injured bird safely.

I had a scare one day with Archie when he disappeared over the horizon. Once I caught up with him, he was sitting on the ground looking sorry for himself. When I called him up to the fist, he tried to come, and sort of bowled over back onto the ground. I instantly knew something was wrong and it was a sickening feeling. He was hanging one of his wings slightly and so I picked him up and took him straight home, feeding him up and keeping him warm. The wing was not completely useless, but was obviously causing him some discomfort; it was hanging maybe an inch lower than the other. I decided the best course of action was to monitor his progress. The

following day, Archie seemed a little better in himself, so I decided to try a couple of short flights of, say, 6ft, to see if he could 'run the injury off' like a sports player might a dead leg. But it was the same problem as before; Archie was trying to fly but it obviously hurt him too much and again he flopped to the grass, squawking in anxiety. It was time for a veterinary visit.

The young vet gently felt along the wing bone, especially around the elbow, which felt a little hot. In the end he concurred with me; he did not think the wing had been broken, but either sprained or badly bruised by a glancing blow, perhaps as Archie chased quarry or was blown a little too fast in the wind. Either way, we decided to keep a close eye on him for a week and see if things improved. Then short flights were the order of the day to work off the injury and get him back to fighting fit condition. It was an annoyance, because I knew that several weeks out of his season were going to be lost in total, but obviously his recovery was the most important thing.

During the week the wing did not seem to hang so badly, and much to Archie's pleasure I fed him up nicely on a big fat rat. At the end of the week I took him for his first tentative flight, and although he squawked and tried to hop towards me rather than fly because the wing was obviously sore, he was definitely making progress. It took another week's worth of coaxing before he was happily soaring again, and of course some time after that to regain true fitness.

The above gives you an idea of the nature of falconry health incidents and accidents. They will come to you eventually, no matter how careful you are, because if you are looking after your bird in the proper manner you will be flying her, and most incidents come in the field. This is also true in the wild; hunting hawks are a danger to their prey, but can also be a danger to themselves. Hunting is a harsh and risky business. It only takes a split second timing error to catch a branch or hit the ground rather than the quarry, which may result in an injury that, although superficial, could prevent further hunting success. This normally means death to the wild raptor, and is why the top predators such as birds of prey, lions, tigers, and so on, seem to spend most of their time sitting around, inactive. If they do not need to hunt, they do not. It is too risky. This fact is also a good reposte to anyone who suggests it is cruel to keep a bird tethered to a bow perch. As long as they are reasonably fed up, a wild bird would be doing exactly the same thing: kicking back in the nearest tree, taking in the sunshine and watching the world go by.

COMMON CONDITIONS

BUMBLEFOOT

An infection of the feet, which can present itself in several forms, including a small reddened area on the foot, a black pinpoint, or hard, crusty patches.

Bumblefoot is mainly caused by poor perches but can be introduced through ill-fitting furniture and puncture wounds caused by the bird's own talons. Providing quality perching which spreads the bird's weight equally goes a long way to preventing this infection, which is awkward to clear up completely. It seems that once a bird has caught Bumblefoot it is more likely to do so again, and many who seem to have made a complete recovery have regular relapses. Antibiotics can treat the infection, and in the most severe cases surgery may be necessary.

FROSTBITE

Caused by exposure to freezing temperatures, this is a condition to be avoided at all costs. If caught in the wings, the bird may lose the affected area which will never grow back, and the bird will therefore be unable to fly ever again.

It would seem that certain species are particularly vulnerable, particularly those from warmer climes. The types of bird regularly affected include harris hawks, lanners and in particular some of the larger eagles.

In the UK it is classically caused by falconers leaving their birds tethered to a perch in the weathering overnight, and getting caught out by an early or late frost. Petty singles (toes) and wingtips are typically affected, and the former can even drop off if the condition is severe enough. The affected wingtips will be covered in blisters filled with a colourless fluid. Immediate veterinary treatment is vital to save the bird, but it is a woeful falconer who discovers his bird has been frostbitten; it is a nasty disease to combat, and on many heartbreaking occasions, just when the affected bird appears to be rallying, it has a sudden relapse. Antibiotics and exercise to promote blood supply are the order of the day.

Birds of prey can catch chills, and the falconer must bear this in mind. Their sinuses are particularly complex and apparently prone to infection. Birds with colds and chills may flick their heads and sneeze ('snurt'). Again, veterinary treatment is advisable.

Keep a close eye on your charge. After a while you will notice instantly when her behaviour is a little out of the ordinary. Do not put your bird into her night quarters when wet; she will struggle against catching a chill and may well 'go low' if you are not careful. I like my bird to get some real rain on him every now and then; as long as it is not too heavy and prolonged, I think it does him good to get a little 'weathered'. I always ensure he is dry and warm when he comes into his night quarters during the season, however. This is when the nights are coldest and, although he is perfectly capable of surviving through the coldest of nights (as long as he is adequately protected and has enough food to keep him going), something like dampness could take him over the edge. It is surprising how quickly a hawk's health can deteriorate in such a situation.

I make no apologies for mentioning diet again here. To keep your hawk in top condition, you must give her quality feed. This will help her to fight off any infections that may come her way. Quality food means not just the somewhat anaemic diet of day-old cockerels. Variety is the order of the day and if your bird can tuck into three different types of food a week, you are well on the way to giving her an excellent balance. During the flying season amounts and types of food will obviously have to be adjusted to prevent her getting too heavy.

THE MOULT

The moult is often not addressed in falconry books and has taken on a somewhat mystical quality for some novice falconers, a problem exacerbated when falconers talk of the moult with dread and a fair degree of bitterness. This is understandable, because the beginning of the moult marks the end of the hawking season and the start of a period of inactivity (certainly for your bird, but also for the falconer). Let us tackle the subject of the moult and deal with

Feather collecting is an important job during the moult. They may come in useful later if imping is required.

Summer displays are fine, but these are not hunting birds; they will stand down and moult out over the winter months.

these myths and misconceptions once and for all. It, along with the hawking season, is all part of the sport, and there are some methods to ease your bird through and promote the best possible feather growth, which in turn will have your bird in tip-top shape for the resumption of training and hunting.

All birds lose their feathers in a roughly annual moult. It is nature's way of keeping the bird in perfect flying condition (rather like regularly servicing an aeroplane).

Unlike ducks, who shed all their flight feathers at once during what is known as the eclipse, your hawk sheds flight feathers one set at a time. Therefore, the 'index' primary of the right wing will be shed and replaced at the same time as the index primary of the left wing, and so on until all feathers have been replaced with clean, shiny new ones. This is a

laborious process and takes around six months to complete, hence falconers' impatience to get the process over with. The moult takes place approximately between April and September and is triggered automatically by the gradual changes of season. Falconers normally try and hurry the moult through by feeding up their bird and standing her down from hard exercise.

But why do falconers need to stop flying at all? We have all seen birds being flown in summer displays, and they seem to be okay.

This is certainly true; your bird could be flown all year round with no ill effects, but it would prolong the moult. Also, birds being flown in displays are not hunting; they are not crashing in and out of undergrowth, tackling quarry or chasing hard. As mentioned, a hunting bird is at risk of damaging itself or its flight feathers, and any feather damage during the moult merely exacerbates the problem. Also, new feathers which are still 'in blood' are easily damaged. If knocked, stress points can later appear in the feather. These are known as fret marks and are liable to be the place where a feather will break. Fret marks can also be caused by a shock to the bird or a sudden reduction in diet.

The summer is also not the ideal time to be hunting. There is abundant cover on both the trees and the ground which protects the quarry, making it far harder to find, and you may have trouble keeping track of your hawk. This is also the time of the year when quarry species are reproducing, and while it simply is not falconry to send your bird after baby rabbits and the like, it will also do her no good. She will become lazy and will refuse bigger, more sporting targets as they present themselves.

At first, standing your bird down for the moult does seem strange. Just as the weather turns nice we stop hawking and make our birds fat and lazy by feeding them up and giving them little exercise for half a year. Then we have to go through the whole training process again in September.

For me, successfully handling the moult relies on my mindset. I view it as an essential part of the sport, just as much a part of each passing year as the longed-for start to the hawking season. It is something to be welcomed. After your hawk has worked hard all season, you can reward her with greater and greater food treats as you gradually start increasing her weight. This in turn will encourage her to start to moult, as will the early spring sunshine she can now enjoy after those long, hard months of frost, wind and rain.

As I write I am sitting in the garden, watching Archie as he sits on his bow perch on the lawn. It is early April, and he was stood down for the moult around three weeks ago. The sun is drenching us; for what seems the first time this year, it has broken through the interminable cloud and covers everything in a warming splash of gold. Away to my right, a robin is singing in the way only a robin can; an incredible tumbling procession of bubbly notes, like a mountain brook winding its timeless way to the sea. This whole scenario is very welcome, even though it does mark the moult. I am sure that Archie

feels the same way. He is sitting, fat and contented, in that comfortable manner of hawks, one foot surreptitiously tucked into his drawers. He has just finished a gourmet dish of chick and beef, and is contemplating taking a dip in the cool fresh water placed in the bath next to his bow perch. The feathers of his back are warm to the touch as he sits like a miniature solar sponge, soaking up every last drop of sunshine. Everything, I am quite sure, is alright in his world.

And for the first time in what seems like ages, my weekends are suddenly freed up. It is no longer imperative to take Archie out on every free day as long as the weather is up to it. The start of the moult marks the start of spring and early summer, probably my favourite time of the year anyway, when British weather – at least for a while – becomes bearable once more and life seems to take on new promise with the advent of each blue sky.

Moult days are less labour intensive for the falconer, especially if his charge can reside in a shelter out of doors. Here, the bird looks after itself and sits in the open air or cover as she wishes. The falconer's only job is to keep up the food and water supply, and to keep the shelter clean once a week. During the balmy summer nights the hawk can spend the night in her shelter, in no danger from overnight frosts, and can be up ready to greet the sunshine hours before she would normally be roused from her night quarters.

These added hours of sun-worshipping can have impressive results on the bird's feathers over the summer. Many shelter-moulted hawks develop a lovely smoky-blue sheen to their adult plumage, courtesy of the sun and rain and little human interference. I think it must be better for birds to moult in shelters, rather than simply on the bow. At least they can flap around in a shelter, have a little fly, get the blood circulation going and keep themselves amused. Indeed, this morning I was watching Archie actually playing in his weathering; those who do not believe birds play ought to see him. He was deliberately throwing bits of stick into the air and then pouncing on them and 'killing' them in a very exaggerated manner, wings spread and looking very fierce. Then he would bend down, pick up the twig in his bill and fling it into another corner to repeat the exercise. This sort of behaviour has got to be good for him, but cannot be offered to the tethered bird.

Tip: do not leave your hawk out in her shelter until the threat of a late frost has well and truly passed; although being in a shelter should enable her to get above frost level, do not take the risk. Similarly, as the summer progresses into training time once more, start the old routine of putting her back into her night quarters; it is easy to get caught out by an early cold snap if you do not.

Even the bird who is blocked out each day and returned to her night quarters in the evening requires far less daily maintenance. Apart from feeding her up and keeping an eye on her, there is little else that needs to be done. Ensure there is some shade for her on the hottest days, though. It is callous to leave one's hawk under the blazing summer sun with no protection, even if she does have a bath present. A little three-sided shelter to cover her when the heat becomes unbearable should not be difficult to construct.

Routine maintenance only is needed during the moult; the less your bird is manhandled, stressed out and annoyed, the better. Many falconers leave their birds completely untouched for the entire six months. I think this is probably preferable, but be prepared for a stroppy bird which has 'gone back' somewhat by the end of the moult. If you have at least been feeding your bird from the fist every day, or picking her up from and putting her back into night quarters twice a day, she will not have forgotten what it is all about. It is all down to personal choice.

Whatever your choice, you will notice a change in your bird when she is fed up and on 'fat weight'. She will be far less vocal and the best thing you can do is feed her as much as she wants to eat and leave her. Many birds, particularly shortwings in their first year, become very obstreperous on fat weight and just want to be left alone. Archie seemed to change almost overnight when his brows became really prominent. This is just another sign of 'growing up' (similar to a moody teenager!). He was also very anti-social, started swearing at us when we ventured too close, and basically just wanted to be left to sit on his perch in quiet solitude.

It is important to remember that during the moult your bird should be disturbed as little as possible. As mentioned earlier, sudden frights or stress can lead to feather damage, and not just through bating, either. If a bird is acutely stressed during this period, she may well 'pinch out' a feather. This means the feather will suddenly be shed before it is fully developed, with much of the feather still inside the quill. A long wait can then be expected before another feather grows in its place. Pinched out feathers can become a real problem, and some birds have a strange habit of growing their feathers to a certain length and then pinching them out, over and over again, for no apparent reason. Some incidents like these have been cured by trying out differing levels of various minerals and supplements, but one buzzard at The English School of Falconry continues to do this all year long. She is quite unable to fly and probably never will again. It is a most frustrating condition, but thankfully rare.

Do not worry about food levels during the moult; your hawk will put on a lot of weight, but will need it to process the whole lengthy business. Beef and other high-protein meats should feature strongly in her weekly diet. Water, too, is especially important at this time of year because of the more intense heat. It will enable your hawk to bowse should she so wish, cool down with a quick dip, or simply water and preen newly grown feathers.

5 FINDING YOUR OWN HAWKING GROUND

Finding your own hawking ground is an essential element of the sport. So why do so many would-be falconers train themselves and their bird, buy and make their equipment – *then* start looking for somewhere to fly their bird? You should determine your hawking terrain before your bird arrives, otherwise you may end up not hunting it at all, and, as discussed, this is morally indefensible.

A word of warning: if you are friendly with another falconer who has his own hawking land, do not assume you can pitch up with him whenever the fancy takes you. Good hawking land is hard to come by and falconers guard theirs jealously; you might well be on your way to spoiling a good friendship if you constantly utilize someone else's hard-won territory. By all means accept an offer of a day's

Once you have found some hawking territory, do not just go rushing in. Assess its potential first to find out how to give your hawk the best opportunities.

hawking and enjoy it, but never rely on the goodwill of others for your hawking. You will need to find a suitable tract of land for yourself. Be self-sufficient.

Sadly, this is easier said than done, at least in the UK at present. In truly rural areas, the gun still rules over most farms, and heed my advice when I say that guns and birds of prey do not mix. There are organized and rough shoots over most of today's farmland, and even if you are fortunate enough to find a farmer who is not bothered about shooting, locals who are will usually get in first to gain the rights over his land. My advice is not to venture onto land where someone shoots unless you can guarantee they are not there. Relying on a shooter's ability to discern between a hawk and a pigeon is not my idea of good falconry practice.

I once ventured onto a lonely farm and found the old farmer fiddling with a combine harvester. I asked him if there was any chance I could fly my hawk over his land and he fixed me with a fierce look. Gazing pointedly at the pheasant release pens I had failed to notice in a nearby field, he spat: 'All hawks should be shot,' before returning to his combine.

Even today, many farmers see hawks as competitors for their precious game birds, and although you may tell them your little hawk could not catch a pheasant if he tried, you will be lucky to get anywhere near. Do not be tempted to lie, either; you will be caught out at some stage and then have to deal with an extremely angry farmer. This reminds me of a classic 'fireside tale':

Two falconers, desperate for hawking territory, convince a farmer that their birds only take rabbits and will not touch his pheasants. Reluctantly, the burly farmer agrees to let them hawk his land.

The pair are delighted and over the following weeks catch several rabbits and the occasional pheasant. These they manage to stash in their Land Rover and enjoy over a glass of wine each weekend.

However, the inevitable happens one Saturday, and just as one of their harris hawks binds onto a hen pheasant, the farmer's pickup comes bumping over the field. Struggling with the birds, one of the red-faced falconers just manages to disentangle the dead pheasant from the talons of his bird as the farmer leaps from his vehicle.

'Bloody hell!' he roars at the pair. 'Them's my bloody pheasants. You said those buggers couldn't catch pheasants!'

'They can't, usually,' the pleading falconers respond. 'It must have been injured.'

Then, with the timing seemingly only reserved for animals, small children and those incapably drunk, the other harris crashes into the undergrowth nearby and comes flapping out into the field with a large cock pheasant. In full view of the apoplectic farmer, it rips off the bird's head.

The falconer, still manfully hoping to resurrect the situation, pulls off his harris, and holding aloft the decapitated game bird proffers it to the farmer.

'Here,' he said placatingly, 'you have this one.'

The two could not get hawking land within a ten-mile radius after that little episode.

When looking for your own hawking ground, you must decide on the type of land you really need. If you plan to hunt longwings you need to live in the right locality. As mentioned, longwings generally need large tracts of open land if they are to be hunted with any degree of proficiency. Do not consider hunting falcons in enclosed territory. If you have the right sort of land nearby, so much the better. You then need to determine whether you intend to pursue rooks on cornfields, or head to the heathland and moors for partridge and grouse.

Shortwings benefit from their ability to adapt to a variety of hawking land; a suitable belt of trees ensures a decent follow on flight, while some well-drained meadows give excellent rabbit territory. A little mixed woodland is nice and can offer some useful shade on a warm day.

Streams and lakes offer excellent opportunities for ducks and waterfowl such as coot and moorhen, but can also be a potential hazard. This is best illustrated by another fireside tale, this one featuring my two old sparring partners, Phil Gooden and Dave Ashton.

On a particularly freezing winter's day, Dave and Phil were hawking near to a small lake when one of their birds dived in and caught a moorhen on an island in the middle. This obviously caused some consternation. Phil suggested Dave take his kit off and

A pond is a real bonus for the ardent hawker; it offers a chance of moorhen, coot or even duck.
However, an island can be a curse. Be prepared to get wet!

go for a swim, seeing as it was Dave's bird which had done the dirty deed.

'Those are the rules, mate,' he said sagely, tucking his gauntlet under one arm and starting to roll a cigarette.

Dave actually considered doing just this; but the fact that there was thick ice across the lake seemed to deter him. With a flash of inspiration, he remembered seeing a boat in the farmyard and started to run back, leaving Phil studiously puffing on his roll-up. When he explained to the farmer what had happened, Dave was told the boat had a hole in it, but the kids might have a rubber dinghy somewhere nearby. Eventually, the party returned to the lakeside and proceeded to pump up the inflatable dinghy. By this time the harris was just starting to tuck into a second helping.

In the end it was Phil who clambered into the untrustworthy vessel ('It just folded up around him like a clam when he sat in it,' Dave later recounted)

and made his way laboriously across to the island, breaking ice as he went. The bird was eventually retrieved, and remarkably both falconers remained dry. (That was to change some time later when a similar situation occurred on a different pond. This time Dave did take the plunge, while Phil stood on the bank laughing.)

Do not turn up at a farm dressed in all your falconry finery, with a bird on your fist. This could be construed as arrogance. Did you think you were just going to get permission and then disappear for a wander with your bird? The best approach is to turn up smartly dressed and politely explain your situation. Tell the farmer what sort of bird you have, what sort of quarry it is likely to take and how it will do so in a very environmentally friendly manner. In most cases, people are fascinated to find out a bit more about birds of prey, and you can take

Fieldcraft should be practised and improved; use available terrain for cover and learn how different species interact.

advantage of this by filling them in on some aspects of the sport. As a trump card, offer to take the farmer out with you and show him how your hawk hunts. I find it is usually best to approach landowners in person rather than on the phone (they are exceedingly difficult to pin down anyway).

Should you be lucky enough to get a favourable response, you need to establish exactly what the boundaries of the land are. It is human nature to believe that the next field or next wood is packed with quarry, but trespassing with a hawk is still trespassing. Apart from the fact that you may upset other farmers and disturb their game, there is also the chance that your bird may come into uncomfortably close contact with shooters. You would have no cause for complaint were your bird shot while you were trespassing. Occasionally, your bird will of course wander onto uncharted land, or even catch quarry adjacent to your territory. In this situation you should retrieve your hawk as soon as possible. If you bump into the landowner who wonders what you are doing, you can only humbly explain and hope he realizes your genuine mistake.

Do your best to look after your shoot and the farmer's interests. You can act as a useful extra pair of eyes for the farmer, noticing a gap forged in a hedge, a broken fence line, a sheep stuck in a ditch. These services will be invaluable to him and will serve you in good stead. He may well recommend your services to another nearby landowner and suddenly your hawking land has expanded by another few hundred acres.

Look after the crops and equipment; do not traipse straight through a newly sown crop as this will not endear you to anyone. Climb fences without leaving great sagging lengths of wire behind. Climb gates at the hinge, where they are stronger, and if you open them to help your progress, always remember to close them behind you.

A message of goodwill or bottle of wine for your generous benefactor at Christmas will also serve you well. In general, I do not think it is necessary to pay for hawking rights; try hard enough and you will find some land of your own. The exception to this could be the hawking holiday. These can be great fun. Get together with a couple of mates and disappear somewhere remote with your birds. Plenty of fresh air, plenty of tall tales, plenty of exciting flights, plenty of good food and plenty of beer are sure to make your trip a resounding success.

FIELDCRAFT

Very little has been written about fieldcraft, yet to me general fieldcraft is second-nature because I was brought up firstly as a wildlife-watcher and then a shooter. Most people simply do not know how to move, talk, hide and observe in the countryside, and these skills have to be learned and practised. Although, by its very nature, falconry is entirely different to shooting, many of the same rules apply. Fieldcraft also includes obtaining an intimate knowledge of your quarry species (see Chapter 7).

The general rules of fieldcraft are simple and obvious when considered.

• Always wear drab-coloured clothing so as not to draw attention to yourself. A cap or similar breaks up the tell-tale human outline nicely and also shades the face (white people have incredibly shiny faces from above; reflections from the sun let birds know you are there. Not convinced? Watch a woodpigeon from under the peak of your cap as it approaches, then lift your face to the skies. It will jink away and speed off immediately).

• Do not wear perfume or after-shave when hawking; rabbits and hares will smell it from a very long distance.

• Never walk straight across a field; you stick out like a sore thumb. Instead, always follow hedge and tree lines for cover and move slowly but deliberately.

• You should, as a conscientious falconer, be aware of the wind direction and speed, but pay particular attention to the way it is blowing as you approach known warrens, otherwise there will be nothing for your hawk to chase when you get there. Remember, in the wild she has no added nuisances like noisy, smelly humans to encumber her performance; she just silently glides in or drops unseen from an overhead bough.

Many falconers are incredibly noisy in the field. Some of this is necessary, such as whistling to the bird or shouting the occasional instruction, but the

In this picture there is a tiny dark spot in the middle of the gateway. It is a rabbit, cowering in the long grass. Would you have spotted it, or would you have stormed past it without noticing? Fieldcraft is essential if you are to succeed regularly.

general uproar caused is a mystery to me. The same falconers then wonder why they never see any quarry. One such individual, who purports to be a true falconer but never hunts his birds, had the gall to tell me: 'There is never any quarry when we go out,' without the slightest hint of embarrassment. There is always quarry there, if you have chosen suitable terrain for your bird; you just have to know how to find it.

In my shooting days I was mainly concerned with hunting with high-powered air rifles, an activity that requires not an insignificant level of fieldcraft to enable you to creep within 30yd of your quarry. Any sort of noise was definitely out of the question. I have brought this style of hunting to my hawking and I believe it makes a difference. The thump of a heavy

footfall gives away your presence; an inopportune cough, loud speech, shuffling feet through long grass, incautious, high-speed marches; all are easily picked up by wild creatures and will reduce your bag. Birds and animals will slip away long before you reach them, and those you do capture are likely to be hunched in hiding, hoping you will pass by, rather than those captured unawares going about their daily business.

Practise picking up your feet and choosing the least noisy routes along leaf-strewn paths and rocky walkways. It will pay off. Train your bird to work with you with the least amount of furore so that you can both work the fields and hedgerows as quietly as possible, like true hunters rather than a noisy rabble.

Other fieldcraft tips that may be useful: when you

quietly approach a field of long grass and you suspect there may be rabbits around, try and position your hawk usefully nearby and use the age-old squeaking technique. This is no joke; if you squeak between pursed lips or on the back of your hand, it sounds very much like a rabbit's distress call. I guarantee that if there are any rabbits in the vicinity, they will sit bolt upright, straining to see where the panic lies. This movement may well be enough to allow your hawk to latch onto their position.

If you are straining to hear, whether because of background noise, wind or distance, cup a hand around either ear. This stereotypical posture is not just affectation; the cupped hands act as bigger ears, trapping more sound and funnelling it down to the earhole.

Get a feel for your hawking ground. Observe it a few times without the added concern of your bird. Visit it at different times of the day and observe where the wildlife is to be found. Where are the woodpigeon flight lines and sitty trees? How far do the rabbits venture from the safety of the warren? Where do the magpies congregate for their 'treetopping' social meets and feeding opportunities? What crops are being sown in the fields this year, and how will that affect wildlife movement? Where are the coppices and spinneys that will house the pheasants and partridges and where will they venture out to feed? Once these questions have been answered satisfactorily, you can set about deciding how you are going to use the topography and different climate conditions to get near the quarry.

6 BUYING AND TRAINING YOUR BIRD

Some might argue that it is a little odd to leave training and its pitfalls until this stage of the book. I would disagree. It is of paramount importance to know as much as you can about birds of prey and their welfare before you contemplate getting one of your own. Once you have made the necessary arrangements for accommodation, food, furniture, healthcare and your own training, and have read up as much as you can about falconry and birds of prey in general, you should be ready, under the watchful eye of an experienced falconer, to take on your own bird.

This chapter deals with the basics of training both long- and shortwings, and outlines some of the pitfalls to avoid. Again, hands-on experience cannot be overestimated. The aims of training are straightforward enough: to get your bird used to you and her surroundings, to get her flying to you when you whistle, to get her flying free, to get her fit – and to get her hunting.

PICKING UP THE NEW BIRD

This is a stressful time, for both bird and falconer alike. The young bird will be spitting, hissing, wild, and the new falconer will, quite frankly, be somewhat overawed. Do not fear; this will pass. It is a necessary hurdle of the sport.

An alternative is to buy an older bird, perhaps already trained and no longer wanted by its falconer, although to my mind this defeats the object of the exercise, which is the pleasure of training and flying your own bird 'from scratch'. If you decide to take this option, make certain that you know the falconer concerned as far as is possible, and can reliably quote the history of the bird. Otherwise, you will have no

idea of its temperament or its health, how it has been trained or treated – in short you will be taking on a completely unknown quantity. Once you have paid for the bird and taken it home, only to realize it is an imprint, or worse, you will have no comeback.

In my opinion, the beginner needs to learn his trade completely, and that means taking on one of this year's birds. If you cannot be bothered to train your own bird, you will not be bothered to hunt it and should choose another hobby.

When choosing your bird, after carefully considering which type would best suit your requirements, pocket, hunting terrain, and so on, some careful checks should be made.

Firstly, make sure your supplier is a reputable breeder, and that you know someone who has used his birds before and would recommend them (this may take some time, but it is imperative not to simply buy your bird from the first person to offer you one). Those breeders with a good pedigree of quality stock are the ones to look for. Unfortunately, as with all businesses, there are crooks in falconry who will sell you anything from injured, diseased or imprinted birds to unreliable furniture and overpriced, inadequate additional equipment. As always, remember the old adage, *caveat emptor*: buyer beware. Your birds should not be taken from their breeding aviary too young otherwise they will imprint (assume you are the parent) on you and you will experience all sorts of problems.

Certain species, such as harris hawks, are relatively easy to breed and you will find there are some falconers who will simply throw them together into an aviary and let them get on with it, looking forward to the rich rewards each chick will bring. Indeed, some fine birds are produced in this way. However, because wild birds are no longer introduced into breeding for falconry in anything like the numbers they used to be, there is a relatively small gene pool for some species. This can lead to later health problems, and some lines of birds have been discovered to have genetically inherited problems, so again, buying from a quality breeder is essential.

Do not part with any money before you have seen the bird and had the chance to look her over properly. You should take care to give her a thorough once over, preferably with the help of a friend who can cast her while you assess her condition. Particular attention should be paid to her feet to check for any sign of bumblefoot: small lesions, a black spot, hard scaly patches or any swelling or reddening of the ball of the foot.

Tip: beware the talons! At this stage of its young life, the hawk will be terrified and will automatically clench its feet on anything nearby.

Check to see that the eyes are wide and alert, and the nasal passages are clean and clear. Is there any major feather damage, particularly fret marks, which will show up as little lines across the quill itself and which may well cause problems through later breakages? Is the inside of the mouth clean and pink, with no foul odour on the breath? Is there an infestation of mites? Does the bird appear to be able to breathe without overdue exertion? Are the bones straight? Can she stand cleanly on both legs? Is either wing drooping at all?

All these things must be checked before you hand over your money, for you are likely to face an inquisition if you later try and claim the bird was not up to scratch. A word of warning: many breeders will expect payment in cash. This is simply the way most transactions are carried out in falconry.

Once you have decided your bird is fit and you are happy to pay for it, you should place it in a travelling box to transport it home. A stout cardboard box will do, as long as there are plenty of air-holes and a strip of carpet inside that she can cling onto. Avoid newspaper, as this will cause her to slip around and hurt herself. The box should be as dark as possible to avoid the hawk crashing around unnecessarily. Once you are home, the next job is to fit her with the necessary furniture. You will again need help to cast

her. Make sure you have a cushion underneath her feet so that she can grip onto it without hurting herself. Take your time and make sure anklets, jesses and leash, bewits and bells all fit comfortably. You do not want to have to cast her again for some time if it can be avoided.

At this stage it is good practice to take the sharp points off her talons with a pair of nail clippers to stop her hurting herself. Her beak should be okay, but may also need a little coping. These tasks should be carried out in a quiet room with as little fuss and noise as possible. You should ensure your new charge cannot crack wings on any hard surfaces as she flaps about. As well as a cushion for her talons, have a clean tea towel handy to wrap around her back as she is cast. Then the sweat in your hands will not remove the natural bloom (and therefore waterproofing) from her feathers. At this stage, falcons can be hooded, although I'm not entirely convinced of the wisdom of this. To my mind, immediate hooding can only prolong the bird's fear and agitation in the presence of the falconer.

Take the bird to her night quarters and leave her to calm down and get over the first few hours of your new partnership. Remember, a hawk cannot be disciplined like a dog or child. Striking or intimidating her can only cause harm. Other, more ancient methods must be employed to get her to understand what falconry is all about.

Some say a new hawk should be left to get used to her surroundings for a week or two before training is started. I am not so sure. Surely the most important thing is to reduce the new and frightened bird's inevitable stress levels as soon as possible? At this stage, she is scared of man and believes him to be a threat. This can only be overcome by initiating her training and making her realize that your arrival is in fact good news as it means possible food and flying. If she is left for a week she will simply spend those days terrified of every movement you make. She will be no less scared of you at the end of the week than she was to start with.

Some birds learn quicker than others. The important thing to remember when training is that it is not a race; take no notice of those falconers who claim to have had their bird catching quarry within a week. Take your time and do it properly. As with the moult, embrace your training period. It is part and parcel of becoming a falconer and you should cherish it, rather than crash through it hoping to get your bird into the air on a solo flight as soon as possible. There will be moments during training that you would rather forget: petulant behaviour on the bird's part (or perhaps, on occasion, yours), and when things go awry. There will also be moments when you are elated due to your last success. All will stick in your mind, especially with the first bird you ever train. Make the most of those moments. They are what this sport is all about.

SHORTWING TRAINING

THE GLOVE

The first stage of training is getting your bird to stand on the glove.

When you pick her up she will be startled and the slightest movement from you will cause her to bate away (hawks tend to do this far more than falcons). Then, stopped short by her leash, she will hang upside down like a bat. Some never really appear to get over this, but most soon realize that it is far easier to remain in the upright position. You must show her how to return to the fist after bating, not by swinging her up like a pendulum, which puts undue pressure on the leg bones, but by gently grasping her back or front and bodily placing her on the fist. (I prefer the back, for then there is no chance of talon damage, accidental or otherwise.) It is highly likely that she will immediately jump straight off your fist again. This is where the falconer's legendary patience must come into play. Every time this pantomime is carried out, you must play your part and replace her on the fist. Be prepared for this to take a long time. In time, your hawk should realize two things: first, that she cannot go anywhere when she tries to bate off the fist; and second, how to regain the fist on her own.

The next step is to offer her food on the fist, and the way in which the food is presented can greatly affect your success rate. The idea is that your hawk will only get her food from your fist at this stage; she will begin to realize that you are the food provider, and therefore not quite as scary as first imagined.

Pull apart a DOC or offer a juicy red piece of beef, slipping it quickly between the pad of your thumb and your forefinger while she sits warily on your fist.

Tip: beware of the feet; hawks forget all etiquette when there is food in sight, and you will be caught by the talons if you are not quick and careful about placing and removing food near her feet. Even the most even-tempered bird in the world will inadvertently 'foot' you in an attempt to get food. I have found the best way of feeding a trained bird on the fist is to offer the food at beak level, which should then be grabbed in the beak. Drag the food (and therefore the bird's head) down quickly and secure the morsel in your hand in one smooth movement, taking care to avoid the feet as much as is humanly possible. If you do it properly you should have no problem.

Traditionally, food should be held in a particular manner in the glove. The meat should not be placed in the fist, but over the pad of the thumb, with the lower three fingers securing it. This feels uncomfortable at first, but is worth persevering with as it makes it easier for your hawk to feed and prevents leash, jesses, and so on, getting soiled with food. At this point, she may well not even deign to look at your tempting offering because she is on such a high weight after coming out of the breeding aviary. Roll the piece of meat gently between your fingers to attract her attention; try tapping her foot gently with it. She may be tempted to put a foot on it and that is an excellent start for you. Alternatively, she may display that wonderful bird of prey apathy and pretend you do not even exist. It is amazing how a hawk will find a blank wall infinitely more interesting than you in such situations. Whatever happens, try not to stare straight at her; as a top predator with two forward-facing eyes you are an intimidating creature and staring unnerves many birds of prey.

If she fails to eat, give her five to ten minutes then remove the meat and end the session. If this does happen it is essential she gets no food that night. The same technique needs to be tried the next day. Very soon your bird will realize that the only way she is going to get any food is to take it from your fist. Do

The correct way to feed a bird on the fist. The meat is held over the pad of the thumb and secured with the lower three fingers.

Tying a hawk onto the bow.

not panic if she refuses to eat for several days; this will not harm her as long as you keep a close eye on her general appearance (beware slitted eyes and a huddled and lethargic attitude, which could denote

she is falling too low). Eventually, her stomach will tell her that the bravado is not a good idea and she will bend her neck to feed. This is a major milestone in your training. Permit yourself a grin, but make sure you are looking away from your hawk so you do not upset her! Offer her as much food as she will take from you that night.

After this, she will begin to learn that good behaviour brings rewards in the form of food. If she does not perform, she does not get a plentiful reward and her weight will be cut back until you find that crucial point where her natural stubborn spirit is overpowered by her hunger. You are then well on your way to finding her elusive flying weight.

You will need to determine flying weight before you can safely fly your bird. When she is on flying weight, she responds to your call immediately in the hope of food because she is hungry; not so hungry that she is weak, but hungry enough to ensure she will come back to you – and hungry enough to want to get out there and hunt.

THE PERCH

The next step in training is to get her used to being picked up from and tied back onto her perch.

At first, this will have to be done before she is properly manned, which makes the process all the harder, but her fear of you will dissipate quickly.

Tip: if you intend to put your hawk in her own shelter so she can fly free, do not do it straight away. In all the excitement and early anxiety of training she may well crash about somewhat and risk injuring herself. Wait until she is much steadier before turning her loose. The period she spends tethered to her bow perch will do her no harm and will prevent any unfortunate early mishaps that may mar your training.

To pick her up, take up the jesses in your right hand and bring them between the thumb and forefinger of your gloved hand. Then you will have to pick up your bird and stand her on the fist (when she is trained, a glove pressed against her shins will encourage her to step on; when one foot is on, the glove should be raised and she will climb on with the other foot). At first she will no doubt hang upside down while you untie the leash, but when this has been overcome you should place her in Safety A and return her to your glove. Again, this process is made much easier when your bird is not flapping wildly around you.

When putting her back on her bow, keep her on your fist above the perch while you tie the falconers' knot, remembering not to give her too much leash in case she bates hard and damages herself. Then gently back her up against the perch so that the backs of her legs touch it. With a little persuasion she should step back onto it. She will soon get used to this routine and you will also do it without thinking.

Tip: practise your falconers' knot until you can do it quickly and efficiently, even in the dark, without having to pause to think about what to do next. If you are nervy and take your time tying down a new hawk, she too will get nervous and may start to flap about. You will then be faced with a greater problem and will get yourself all worked up over something that should take just seconds.

MANNING

The next step is manning; simply taking your hawk out into her surrounding environment and getting her used to everyday occurrences so that she will not be disturbed when she encounters them while flying free.

Hawks are renowned for being stubborn when it comes to this stage, and take an age to get used to you and your environs. Falcons, on the other hand, usually pass with flying colours. Never fear, though; they usually make up for it in another way!

Your hawk must get used to standing comfortably on the fist, and you must get used to providing a comfortable perch. You should persuade her not to be 'rude' and turn her back on you as she stands on the glove. A hawk should always face the falconer on the fist where practicable. At first she may well turn the other way, not knowing any better, but you need to coax her round. This is best achieved by gently pushing her tail at the base. This will usually encourage her to turn, although there may be birds that need moving bodily round. Soon enough she will realize there is no point facing the other way because she cannot see you and any potential food, and will suddenly cease to do so.

When carrying a bird on the fist, your arm should be kept at roughly a right angle to your body, with the elbow tucked into your hip to prevent any strain

Manning walks help your hawk to get used to you – and her surroundings.

on your back. At first this will seem strange to you both, but after a while it becomes second nature. Try and ensure your arm remains steady at all times, even if the terrain you are walking over is uneven. In this way, your bird will know she is safe on your arm. You know you have achieved a truly steady ride when she can safely travel with one leg tucked up!

THE CAR

Introducing your hawk to the car is another step in the process, and you can begin by enticing her to enter her travelling box by throwing a titbit in for the first few times. She will soon hop in eagerly without needing this enticement. Progress to starting up the car while she sits in it and work your way up to going for a short ride. Most birds adapt well to travelling,

while a few simply cannot. If your bird is car sick, do not persist in taking her; dehydration can rapidly occur if a hawk starts to vomit. If you plan to travel a long distance, make sure you keep regular checks on your bird. Beware other packages and cases blocking the travel box air-holes.

Once she is comfortable in your presence and happily feeds off the fist even if there is activity nearby, it is time to start the long road to free flight.

STEPPING UP

Now you want to encourage her not only to feed from your garnished fist, but to step up to greet you, which will then stop her bating away from you as you approach. Again, this marks a turning point in your relationship, and things start to get a little calmer

A young female kestrel fluffed up to keep out the morning chill.

The ferruginous buzzard is a striking bird and one of my personal favourites.

With experience, your bird will learn to read the wind like a map and use it to fly effortlessly.

The thrill of watching your hawk come to the fist never diminishes; it is, quite simply, why falconers persevere.

Harris hawks can be flown in groups, greatly adding to the 'carnival' atmosphere of hawking with these amicable predators.

Most birds are now captive-bred, and many have to be hand-reared early in their development. It can prove a messy business!

Babyish petulance is written all over the face of this youngster, on one of his first solo-flying forays.

The ubiquitous harris hawk; this bird is in mature plumage.

Education is the key to the future of our sport. We must continue to teach and encourage a love of the countryside and a knowledge of all that is in it.

The seconds before a stoop are particularly exquisite. What has the bird seen? Will it decide to plunge,
or has it mistaken a leaf blowing in the wind for the stealthy escape of a rabbit?

Streaking across a field of young rape, this harris is hot on the heels of a buck rabbit that exploded from the hedgerow.

A falcon at rest is beguiling. Foot tucked away and only the occasional movement of the head giving her away, it is hard to imagine she can stoop at estimated speeds well in excess of 100mph.

from now on when your new charge does not flap and squawk each time you approach.

This stage is usually achieved without too much difficulty. When you approach her, kneel in front of her perch and bring your garnished fist up to her feet. All being well she will try to grab some meat. Once one foot is on the glove, gently lift up your fist. She will then hop on board with the other foot. If for any reason she does not seem bothered, her weight needs to be cut. It is normally a fairly straightforward affair, however, and she may well be able to move to the next lesson in the same training session. If your hawk is a quick learner, then by all means let her go ahead, but do not be tempted to rush her onto the next stage before she is completely ready. If you do this, it will catch up with you in the long run. Better to take things slowly and patiently, fully aware that your hawk has mastered each passing lesson.

JUMPING

Once stepping up has been grasped, it is time to convince her to jump a short distance to you.

Place her on her bow perch or block, and, tying her leash to the ring on your glove, offer her a tasty morsel around 6in from her feet and give a low whistle (if you cannot whistle, buy one). From now on you should always whistle during her training. A whistle in a different tone can later be used to get her to 'follow on'.

Tip: in training sessions, always ensure the offering is a morsel, such as a leg or head of chick, rather than the whole thing. A hungry bird coupled with a nervous falconer is likely to end with the entire day's rations wolfed down at the start. This will not increase the chances of your training success.

Your bird should show signs of wanting to come, perhaps parading up and down her perch or stretching her neck in an effort to try and reach the food, or making some frustrated vocalizations. Do not let her get at the offering! Eventually, she should get the message and hop the short distance, where she can have a taster as a reward. Then you can replace her and try again, perhaps extending the distance just a little bit (do not overdo it and put her off too soon). Again, you may find she takes to this

like a duck to water and is jumping leash-length straight away. If so, great; repeat it once or twice, let her have a reward, and feed her up for the day, leaving her to put over her crop in peace. If she does not jump to you after a reasonable amount of time, then it is no more rations. She can try again tomorrow when she may be a little more inclined to make an effort. Once this mission has been accomplished, you will need to increase the distance she is jumping, until she will happily leap the distance of the leash the first time your offer food and whistle.

And on we go, taking small steps and continuing the learning curve without a pause. Your hawk should move seamlessly from one stage to another, not realizing that with the passing of each day she has learned a subtle new lesson. In this way, her learning is so gradual as to seem a natural transition.

At this stage, before you progress to the use of the creance, we should discuss the all-important falconry factor – wind.

Wind plays a big part in the life of most creatures, but particularly in those of birds. In the wild they obviously have to learn to adapt to this factor quickly, but falconers must bear in mind that their charges have little or no experience of wind, mostly being born in the relative shelter of secluded aviaries. Because of this, your hawk will need to learn about wind on her own, so you should not take her out when it is gusting too hard. Later, she may be able to handle stiffer breezes, but certainly during early training you should make sure the weather is not too rough for her.

Naturally, birds sit facing the wind (this is to keep their feathers streamlined and therefore ensure they maintain maximum body heat). They also take off and land into the wind because it is much easier to do so. When carrying your hawk, you should always be aware of the wind direction and how she is sitting. You will find she will naturally shift position on your fist to face 'the wind. Do not force her to sit the wrong way round on the fist if a stiff breeze is blowing; it will only upset her and a battle of wills will result, ruining both your days.

At this stage in the training the creance comes into play. This, if you remember, is the thin line used to train your hawk on the wing; light enough so that she is barely aware it is there, but strong enough to stop her if things go awry and she heads for the hills.

CREANCE TRAINING

Your creance training needs to be done in a large open space. You will need access to an area of short grass, without protrusions which the creance could snag on. If this occurs, it can badly upset a hawk's progress. It must be very frustrating for her to take that leap into space (representing the furthest she has ever flown in all probability), then suddenly to be yanked backwards within grabbing distance of her reward. So take care to find a suitable open space with perhaps a line of fence posts to act as a launching-off point but no nearby trees she may be persuaded to head for.

When it is time to train (remembering your charge must have cast and should not have any food in the crop either), attach the creance to her swivel using the same falconers' knot you would normally use to tether her to the bow perch. This is fiddly because the creance is so fine, but you will master it with practice.

Back up your bird onto a handy post, and then walk slowly away, unwinding your creance as you go. Some birds are so keen that before you have walked more than a few paces, they are off the post and heading for you. If this occurs, stick out your fist and give her a little reward. This problem normally sorts itself out, but if she persists in leaping at you before you can get away, you may need the assistance of a friend who can hang on to her until you are ready.

You should be able to tell immediately whether your hawk is going to come on the creance; at first it is likely that she will need a little cut back in rations, because she will probably be absorbed by her completely new surroundings. But if she is going to come, she will be watching your every move – like a hawk.

You must remember to stand on the end of your creance, just in case your hawk decides to try a fly by. Then you will be able to prevent her disappearing over the horizon, unravelling your creance as she goes.

Do not expect her to come further than around 6ft at first. Present your morsel and give her a whistle. The same procedure as before now applies: give her

a minute or two to comply with your request, then if she is not responding her rations must be reduced to sharpen her focus. If she comes to your fist, reward her well and gradually start to increase the distance. Creance training is best done over several sessions, slowly increasing the distance between you each time. Give her a good reward when she does well, and always remember to place her furniture in Safety B as soon as she has landed on the fist. This will ensure she does not dash in, grab her food and dash out again. If she does try it, she will always come up short, and so should eventually learn not to bother.

This 'smash and grab' habit must not be tolerated, for it will follow her into the hunting field where it will become very difficult to correct. When she eventually catches something, if she is physically able, she will disappear into a tree with it to eat it in peace, without any intervention from the approaching falconer, no matter what his protestations.

THE LURE

At this stage, the training of long- and shortwings begins to differ significantly. Some falconers introduce only longwings only to the lure; others say both long- and shortwings should be shown the lure, for although shortwings normally respond to the fist alone, it is useful to be able to attract them should they be a long way away. This makes some sense, and certainly it can do no harm, though it has never seemed necessary for harris hawks. The choice is yours.

As mentioned earlier, the lure is primarily used to first exercise falcons, then call them back to the falconer once they are flying free. The traditional lure is a pair of dried rook's wings (though any other bird's wings can be used), but these days it is more likely to be a horseshoe-shaped piece of leather, stuffed to give it weight and tied to a line. Meat is tied to the lure and it is swung around the falconer in a manner designed to emulate the movements of quarry trying to evade capture (hence falcons being the main recipients of the lure, since their prey consists mainly of birds). It is an effective means of getting a bird fit, and calling her in when she has travelled some distance from you. Swinging the lure is also an art form in itself.

This little owl demonstrates training on a creance.

Go to a local bird-of-prey centre or display at a nearby fair and watch the falconers swing the lure for their falcons. The really good ones make it look deceptively easy.

You may have seen the lure used at a bird-of-prey demonstration. The falcon comes stooping in at a fair old lick and your breath is taken away when the lure is whipped out of her reach at the last minute and she speeds through and throws up into the air again – but it cannot be that difficult, can it?

To become a proficient master of the lure, you need to dedicate hours and hours to practising. You will develop blisters from the line as it passes over your finger at speed and causes friction. Your arm will ache until you feel as though it will drop off. Perseverance is the key and you must never consider putting a falcon up and starting her lure exercise without being absolutely confident in your ability; your bird can be killed by the lure if she hits it incorrectly. Remember, patience is the skill of the falconer.

The aim of the exercise is to keep the lure just in front of the bird, and when she stoops for the final kill, keep it out of her talon grasp. In this way she will soon put on muscle and will learn to try and try again – useful in the field when quarry evades a first stoop.

There are two basic lure techniques. Firstly, when the falcon is coming in towards you to take its target, gently swing the lure round at your side in a clockwise motion and fire the lure out towards her as she approaches. At the same time, pull it back in front of her, turning through 180 degrees and sending her whistling past you.

The second technique is used if the hawk is directly overhead and meaning to stoop vertically. Swing the lure above your head like a helicopter to ensure she cannot get to it. This sounds easy enough, but try swapping from one method to the other and back – quickly. You will do well not to wrap the entire thing round your neck and give yourself a black eye.

Many books have tried to demonstrate the art of lure-swinging via photos or drawings, but, as with the falconer's knot, I do not think this is a truly feasible option for the beginner, so I will not try. After practising the two lure swings outlined above, find a falconer to teach you, or better still enrol on a longwing course and learn from an experienced falconer. There is no substitute for this; you need an experienced lure-swinger to tell you when you are getting it right, or indeed wrong. Your weaknesses will become glaring when you are up against your first falcon.

Getting the knack is like riding a bike: once learned you will not forget, and obviously the more you practise, the better you will become. Again, I reiterate the importance of having become competent *before* starting to train your falcon. Your bad habits will merely be passed on to her. If she continually catches the lure, she will think the game is too easy and will refuse quarry in the field once she has stooped at it once.

The lure can first be introduced to the hawk or falcon when she receives her daily rations, preferably just before or at the start of creance training. Attach the rations to the lure and approach her so she can see you. A quick whistle and the lure should be swung by your side a few times. Then throw it out in front of her so she can eat her meal from it. In this way she is getting used to the lure and associating it immediately with food.

Shortwings can be introduced to the dummy bunny at this stage, although it can also wait, without great detriment, until she is flying free. Again, meat is attached to it and when the hawk is flying free it can be dragged suddenly from the undergrowth to encourage the hawk to chase and grab it, therefore getting the bird used to the sudden appearance of game. At this stage, simply showing the rabbit and tossing it in front of the hawk with food should suffice to make an early impression.

You will find that during creance work, you will start to detect a more definitive flying weight in your bird and will learn more about how rations will increase

As well as being an expert in handling leather and using tools like these, you will also need to add a little woodwork and some meteorological experience to your armoury!

and decrease her weight, not forgetting factors such as weather, exercise, and so on. Again, this side of falconry is something that can only be gained by hands-on experience, although you should refer to an experienced falconer for guidance.

As a general rule, your hawk will lose weight more rapidly if the weather is especially cold or if she has been pressed into hard exercise. Therefore you must take these factors into account in the amount you feed her. This sounds terribly complicated, but do not fear; with a little guidance you will soon surprise yourself how accurately you will be able to turn the amount of meat before you into pounds and ounces on your bird. As well as a degree of expertise in leather work and carpentry, it would therefore also be useful to have a little meteorological experience if you are determined to turn yourself into a fine falconer! Taking note of the weather is something

Snow makes for picturesque hawking, but cold nights mean extra rations for your bird.

Your bird needs experience of flying into, and out of, trees. She will eventually learn to use them in her hunting techniques.

you should start to do on a daily basis at this stage if you do not already. Cold snaps can take your bird perilously low in condition overnight.

As training is now taking place outside on the creance, the weather will play a part here, too. Wind and rain are not conducive to shortwing flights, as already briefly mentioned. Most falcons can handle a stiff breeze, but at this stage in their training it is better to wait patiently for a calm, clear day.

Once in your training field, when you place your bird on her fence post and whistle as you turn back to her, you want to see a prompt response. It will not do for your bird to decide to fly to your fist only when she has preened, roused, watched a flock of pigeons pass overhead and picked at her jesses. If she is not responding quickly to your whistle, her rations need to be cut. Remember to keep a chart (perhaps on the blackboard in your mews) recording her different weights. You will notice that her attentiveness in the field directly correlates with this.

When she will come like an arrow immediately to your fist over the distance of the creance – usually

around 50yd or so – she is on the verge of her maiden unhindered flight, the next milestone in falconry. Do not get too worked up about this (although I hardly slept a wink before Archie's first free flight!). To this point, providing there have been no hiccups with the creance snagging on anything, your hawk has been totally unaware that she is attached to you by that strong line; you are the only one aware that once that is gone, she is quite capable of disappearing into the blue. As far as she is concerned, she has been capable of that all along, but hopefully has not tried it. Before this monumental training session, however, there is an extra step you should take to ensure that no unforeseen last-minute glitches ruin your carefully laid plans.

Your hawk will probably never have been in a tree in her life and will need to be tested on them to ensure she will come back when asked, just in case she decides to leap into one!

For your tree session you need to find a very particular branch, one that will not cause undue problems by snagging her creance and leaving her

Falcons are usually carried into the field hooded.

Do not attempt your maiden voyage if there is any chance of bad weather, particularly heavy wind. Assess the situation first and make your decision sensibly, but do not put off this moment unnecessarily.

dangling by her jesses. The branch needs to be relatively horizontal and comfortable for her to perch on, low enough so that you can back her onto it from the ground, and clear of any other branches your hawk can easily leap to nearby. If she succeeds in doing the latter, her natural inclination will be to get to the top of the tree, and she will ladder up the branches, winding her creance round them as she goes. This is most definitely not what you want, for if she tries to fly to you, an enormous tangle is the inevitable result and you will be forced to climb the tree to try and fetch her down.

Back her onto your carefully chosen perch and unwind the creance, remembering not to keep it too taut. Walk away some 15yd and turn to give your whistle. Hopefully she will dive towards you, but do not be too upset if this strange new perspective on the world is a little more alluring than your pick-up piece of meat. Only a cut in weight will persuade her otherwise.

When she comes to you willingly from the tree, the moment has finally arrived. The night before your maiden flight, cut her rations ever so slightly just to ensure she is 'sharp set' for the big day. And try and get some sleep yourself.

THE MAIDEN VOYAGE

It is not unusual for the novice falconer to continually put off the maiden voyage.

He has just started to get on really well with his new charge, after what is usually a rather ignominious start to their relationship. The bird is genuinely pleased to see him (or should be) when he approaches the mews and is keen to get out on the training ground. She is also well manned enough to behave nicely when guests and visitors come round to admire her. The falconer is getting enjoyment from her because she is making almost daily progress.

Then, on the fateful day, a look out of the window reveals some clouds on the distant horizon, and the falconer, eager for an escape route, decides discretion is the better part of valour. 'Don't want to risk it,' he thinks, and goes about his business.

This is an honourable thought, if indeed there is bad weather on the way, for you definitely do not want to 'risk it'. But if you continually put the moment off, it will become increasingly hard to make the step; your bird will lose condition, you will lose faith and time will pass you by. Before long, you will be well into the hawking season when you should be out enjoying yourself in the field instead of fretting over the first flight. Then, if you are not very careful, you will suddenly be well on your way to becoming one of those deplorable falconers who does not hunt his birds, but merely keeps them for show.

Ironically, the self-same reticence to take the bird out slowly disappears from many novices when they successfully overcome the first few solo flights. Then, when they experience the thrill of hawking, they start to push their luck and take their bird out in increasingly bad weather. It is more likely the bird will be lost at this time rather than early on. Of course, I would be lying if I said I was not affected by this. However I received a short, sharp shock. I was lucky.

A month or so after I got Archie flying free and following on, the weather took a turn for the worse late one week. Having been working on a regional newsdesk all week, I had spent much of it taking sly glances out of the window at the unseasonably blue sky. Then, on Thursday, along with my mood, the skies darkened, rain swept in and the wind got up. Typical. Just as the weekend approached.

On Saturday morning the weather was better than I had expected it to be, although a steady spatter of rain blotched the car windscreen. I got Archie from his night quarters, and against my better judgement, started to collect my hawking stuff together. By the time I had put Archie in the car and driven the couple of miles to my nearest hawking ground, the rain had abated, although the clouds still looked ominous. Archie was getting fitter and fitter and had embarked on a couple of decent chases the last time we had been out. I decided I could do with the exercise and was tempted to go for it.

As soon as I took off his furniture and let him go, I realized I was being stupid. The wind whipped him away to the other side of the field where he turned and, like a man wading through treacle, battled until he managed to grab onto a branch and held tight until I got there. It was something of a surprise to him to encounter wind, this unseen yet formidable opponent, yet he handled it remarkably well; I would guess that birds have at least some inherited flight knowledge. By the time I had stomped across the width of the field of knee-high grass, it was raining again and Archie was looking at me like I was mad. Then, something caught his eye and in a blink he disappeared.

I ran to my right just in time to see his worryingly small form flip over the hedge at breakneck speed. I caught one more glimpse of him on the other side, wings splayed and looking as though he was on a rollercoaster and hanging on for dear life. Then he was gone. My heart sank. The rain spattered down noisily on my cap and dripped from the peak as I blew shrilly on my whistle and strained for another glimpse of the hawk. Nothing.

I belted across the field and scrambled through the hedge as the heavens really opened and it started raining in a very consistent, heavy manner. Despite my repeated whistles and shouts, and waving a DOC to every bird within several miles, I did not see Archie for twenty minutes. I was soaked and absolutely appalled at what I had done. Until you have been through the feeling of having lost your bird (which you inevitably will at some stage, but hopefully only for a short while) you cannot know how desolate it is. You feel empty. After all that preparation, training, effort, patience, even expense – nothing. For a further five minutes I searched, occasionally stopping under the lee of a hedge or oak and listening for the tell-tale sounds of corvids (crow family) getting excited about something. But the wind was too strong and was starting to roar; realistically Archie could have been ten miles away by now. I decided to head home, phone round all and sundry in case he was spotted, get some genuine wet weather gear and get back out here. I headed to the car.

It was only as I climbed the last stile next to the parked car that I saw him. He was sitting, screened from the worst of the wind, on a fence post next to the vehicle. He was watching me with interest. Inevitably, as relief flooded through me, I asked him, 'Where have you been?' He declined to tell me, but instead shook rainwater from his feathers in an explosive rouse which sent droplets pinging away on either side and his leg and tail bells merrily tinkling.

You must encourage your bird to 'follow on', meaning that they will keep an eye on you as you walk ahead, catch up and land in a tree further along the hedge.

He cheerfully hopped onto my fist and back into his travelling box. Safely back at home and tethered to his bow perch, he was given a generous helping of chicks and mice. I determined, for my own punishment as well as to make sure he was okay, not to fly him again for several days – and certainly *never* again when the slightest doubt entered my mind about conditions. As I said, I was lucky; chances are you will not be.

If the weather is fine, with not too much of a breeze, then it is time to undertake this momentous step. Remember, your bird has no idea this is a big day. For her, it is just another training session in the field.

Make sure there is no-one else with you, although there is no doubt that friends and relatives will be anxious to see the big moment. There will be plenty of opportunity for that later. Now is not the time to introduce strange factors to her, just before she takes her biggest step.

When in your training field, remove her leash, swivel and jesses and replace them with field jesses if you do not favour the permanent type.

Tip: put the pieces of furniture somewhere safe where you can get to them quickly. The last thing you need to discover is that you have lost any of her vital equipment. If you place them in a pocket, make sure it is not one you use regularly, as inevitably you will pull out your hand on one occasion and lose a swivel or jess.

Set her on her fence post and turn and walk away. Force yourself to walk 20yd or so without looking back (I have to admit, every step is agony!) and turn. With your usual whistle, present your morsel of food for her (make it a good, juicy piece).

You will never forget the feeling as, with eyes fixed unwaveringly on your fist, she comes completely unfettered to you. Congratulations! Allow yourself a huge grin.

Once this has been achieved, give her a good reward and leave her back on her bow perch or in her shelter. There is no point making her repeat the exercise endlessly. You have reached another major milestone and now you need to get your bird fit and ready to tackle quarry.

INCREASING FITNESS

Your newly trained bird (and yourself) are keen to get out and do some flying. But she has not flown more than 50 or 60yd in her life and has seen little of what the countryside has to offer. It would not be fair to expect her to dash out and start bringing down bagfuls of game. She needs several weeks to get really fit, put on some muscle and start to learn a few tricks of the trade. The quarry she will be attempting to catch will not have been wrapped in cotton wool all its life; it was born in the wild and has learned to survive. Therefore it is no easy target and it is going to take some catching.

The first thing you need to do is to get your bird 'following on'.

This term is used to describe the most common form of shortwing hunting. Basically, you go for a country walk, hoping to spot or ambush some quarry along the way. The falconer wanders forward and calls up his bird who responds by flying past him and landing on a suitable vantage point a little further on to scan the landscape. They move on in this way across their hawking terrain until quarry (perhaps a rabbit or pheasant) is flushed by a dog or falconer, or the hawk herself spots something and goes crashing in after it.

The falconer should start by getting his bird used to moving in and out of trees and 'casting' her to the highest vantage points to give her a good 'bird's-eye view' and also height from which she can stoop.

Your hawk should show little difficulty in using trees, indeed she should positively enjoy it, clambering about on the branches and getting a whole new perspective on life. Casting is the action the falconer makes when giving her impetus to leave the glove. It is done by firmly moving the arm forward, encouraging her to fly. It feels a little awkward at first, but soon becomes second nature. It is possible to cast your bird extremely accurately after a little practice, getting her to land on specific branches that offer the best lookout points.

Tip: the flying jesses can be used in a careful catapult motion to give more impetus to the cast. Obviously, this has to be done with care, not excessive force. Holding the jesses in Safety B, the falconer casts the bird and uses the jesses to give that little extra snap to the movement before releasing them and the bird.

When getting used to casting, take it slowly and do not try to hurl your bird straight away. Take slow steps up to an all-out cast and the hawk should get used to the idea. Remember to always cast her into the wind.

Your training should now become more and more enjoyable for the pair of you, as daily walking sessions on your hawking land are now the order of the day. The length and physical exercise of these country walks should be gradually stepped up to keep your hawk's fitness training going.

To get her started and used to following on, make sure there is a tree beyond you that she can easily fly to. You should give her a short follow on whistle, different from a usual food whistle, but should not show her food and then whip it away at the last minute. This is likely to peeve her somewhat, and may result in her starting to delay her response time to you; after all, if someone kept 'crying wolf' at you, you would not bother to keep responding. Encourage her to fly towards you on your whistle. You may need to raise your fist to get her moving, and as soon as she nears you, drop your arm. Seeing no food for her, your hawk will continue on past you and should avail herself of the next tree in her sight. She has started to learn to follow on.

From here, you can repeat the exercise again, this time offering her a tiny pick-up piece as her reward. You can continue this process, gradually increasing the distance you cover between pick-up pieces. During your hawking forays, only ever give her small pick-up pieces. You do not want to give her too much, for this may take the edge off her hunger and reduce her effective working capability.

Broadwings are usually very alert and alive to their surroundings on these walks. Ideally, your hawk might now take some interest in passing quarry and will be watching falling leaves and kicked stones with deadly interest. The chances are, however, that she will need a little more coaxing to realize she is capable of taking some of this quarry.

While her fitness is being honed by increasingly longer flights, keep an eye on her behaviour to discourage any future problems. Landing on the ground is not ideal, and if your hawk should take to doing this, pick her up and cast her into the nearest tree every time.

She will catch nothing by sitting on the ground and will have to learn that her place is up as high as possible for tactical reasons. Obviously, if you are crossing huge, open tracts of land with no trees, she will need to sit somewhere, but let her use your fist on these occasions so she does not get used to returning to the ground every few metres.

At first, she will not be able to fly far because, quite simply, she is not strong enough. This is usually

Landing on the ground should be discouraged; height is an essential ingredient for success.

demonstrated when your bird becomes reluctant to fly to you, or stops halfway to drop to the ground and squawk petulantly. The beginner must beware of mistaking tiredness for lack of attention and subsequently cutting back her weight, thus compounding her weakness. Small and gradual increases in distance will do the trick until she is capable of flying a couple of miles with ease. Now is the time to sharpen her appetite for the chase. Cue your dummy bunny.

The dummy bunny is an excellent tool for pushing your shortwing in the right direction and getting her used to seeing furry bundles come sprinting from the nearest cover. Usually, the shortwing gets the idea straight away and needs little introduction to the lure; the natural instinct to chase takes over. You will probably only need to use it a handful of times before you are both itching to find the real thing.

You may need some assistance with the dummy bunny. You can walk along as usual, getting your bird to follow on and take in the countryside. Suddenly, an enthusiastic colleague can run for their life as you near them, dragging the bunny behind them on the creance. You should attach some meat to the dummy so that when your bird catches it (which she will do with ridiculous ease, no matter how much you sprint and turn) she will realize it is worth her while.

A country walk can take on a whole new meaning when you have several dummy bunnies laid out in ambush!

The swing lure could prove useful here as a means of encouraging your hawk to take feathered quarry as well. A well-rounded hawk is, I suspect, more likely to take a wide range of quarry, offering you a better day's sport if there are no rabbits to be found. When your hawk is 'feeding up' on a dummy bunny, you can also practise making in and switching her allegiance from the caught quarry to your fist, although this is never quite the same as the real thing. When your bird has really caught a wild, struggling, juicy prey, she is inevitably more reluctant to give it up and you will have to deal with her and then try to craftily slip the quarry into your game bag without her seeing – not as easy as it sounds!

This reminds me of one particularly hawking trip I know of. I cannot, for reasons which will become obvious, name names, but the essence of the story will speak for itself . . .

It was a cold and clear December day and I had been invited on a VIP trip out hawking. Held on a large country estate, the get-together allowed each member of the party a harris hawk to fly and the best of guides as a high-brow PR exercise. Among the gathered throng were various members of the great and good, squires and lords of the manor and a select few members of the press from some prestigious London magazines.

The morning's hawking was extremely enjoyable, and although the large number of guests meant that most quarry knew we were approaching a mile away, we saw a good couple of dog-fights with squirrels in a spinney and a breathtaking display of power from one of the biggest female harris hawks. Sitting on a bow of a willow, she failed to see a large brown hare get up from under her feet and set off at a leisurely lope across a field. Thanks to our shouts, she caught sight of the hare and launched herself at it, gathering pace with rhythmic, powerful beats of her strong wings. The hare, still not unduly perturbed, turned and headed back for the cover of the hedge, and the hawk, realizing her mistake, cut the corner and closed the gap.

With each member of the party having a superb view of the chase, the outcome was hotly debated. As it happened, both bird and hare reached the hedge at the same time and, with a short stoop, the female ploughed in with a whack. We ran along the hedge to see the result. Personally, my money was on the hare weaving through the hedge, leaping the stream on the other side and sprinting away across the next field.

However, a very different scene greeted us when we arrived. The female was in the stream, barely staying afloat as she held the huge hare under the water. As we watched in disbelief, she waited until his struggles subsided before rowing herself and her prize ashore. It was an impressive display of power, for the sodden hare must have weighed in excess of five or six pounds.

The lunchtime snack and pint in a local hostelry was animated, and after a good morning's sport we looked forward to more of the same. It turned out to be not quite as we expected.

After an hour of searching the hedgerows, the very same bird suddenly sat up and stretched her neck, peering into the distance intently. We could see nothing untoward. She set off purposefully, and despite the repeated whistling and yells from the falconers present, disappeared across a field and beyond a tall clump of conifers. We waited expectantly and suddenly, carried waveringly on the wind, came a noise that sounded as if the evil hordes had finally descended and were taking great glee in wreaking earthly havoc.

With bewildered glances, two of the falconers set off at a run across the field and they too disappeared into the clump of conifers. The gathered guests took the opportunity to rest on their shooting sticks and have a quick draft from their hip flasks. Suddenly, the noise doubled and the falconers appeared, sprinting across the field at an impressive pace. As they neared, the red-faced pair yelled at the party to move on quickly around the hedge. One of them was clutching a black bundle under one arm and an irate harris hawk under the other. It was not until we had moved to a safe distance that we finally understood what the commotion was all about.

Somewhat sheepishly, the head falconer explained that behind the clump of conifers was a small freeholding. When they had arrived, the big female harris was perched atop a large chicken run, occasionally diving against the overhead netting and sending the chickens inside stark raving mad. Just as they neared the coop, wondering why the farmer had not appeared with his gun at the sound of the almighty ruckus, things took a turn for the worse. The female found a gap in the netting.

With a triumphant swoop she plunged into the throng and selected the biggest bird – a magnificent black cockerel, obviously the general of the hen army which was now thrashing itself into a frenzy in a collective attempt to escape the winged death. She dispatched him in an instant and set about plucking her prize. Wrestling with the sizeable cockerel and the peeved harris, the falconers grabbed them and legged it back to us. The cockerel was duly hidden and the party moved off, somewhat subdued. No doubt the head falconer's thoughts were centred on the fact that one of the photographer and reporter teams present was from *Farmer's Weekly* magazine.

ENTERING

Now is the time to think about getting your bird entered. Hopefully by this stage, you should have a good working knowledge of her flying weight and she should be showing signs of wanting to chase. Indeed, she may end up helping you out by entering herself. On one of your regular trips, she may well surprise a rabbit or dive on a weasel before you know it and suddenly make you a true falconer. However, most birds need a little longer to finally get the hang of catching prey.

It is up to you as the falconer to make sure your bird has the best chance of catching quarry. This obviously depends partly upon your hawking terrain, but also on how much homework you have done. In an article I wrote for a shooting magazine several years ago, I maintained that every hour spent on reconnaissance with a pair of binoculars had direct results on the bag at the end of the day. The same applies to falconry. Where are the rabbits on your land? What time of day is best to catch them? How can you approach them so they get no sight, sound or smell of you? Where can you find pheasants, or surprise a covey of partridges? Information on aspects of this type of fieldcraft will be dealt with in Chapter 7, but the point is, you need to offer your inexperienced hawk the best possible chance of ending a good chase successfully, and not just wander around in the hope that she catches something. You need to be proactive. If she keeps chasing but has little chance of catching, she will soon begin to believe it is not worth her while and you will have a job to convince her to resume hunting. In the old days, falconers used to use bagged quarry (literally prey caught and placed in a sack, so that when released, the hawk could easily catch it). Thankfully, this practice has been made illegal. Try and enter your bird on a young or inexperienced rabbit. The last thing you want her to do is latch onto a big old buck and get involved in a fight. This could well put her off for life. Likewise, a cock pheasant can put up a spirited defence and so should be avoided for the first few catches if at all possible.

A hawk that catches quarry relatively early in its career usually goes from strength to strength and should become a very competent hunting bird indeed, offering you hours and hours of hawking pleasure.

When she finally catches, make in quickly to dispatch the quarry before any major battles occur. Allow her to have a good cropful and then give her a reward on the fist. Do not fly her again that day. Repeat this exercise for the next few kills and she will feel more comfortable, knowing you are not going to rob her of her hard-earned prize. Again, at this stage, allow yourself a grin. You are now a falconer and should be proud to be one. You have trained your shortwing, looked after it, helped it first to fly free and then to hunt successfully. Now, as long as you maintain your discipline and look after your bird's welfare, you should have many months of pleasure ahead.

LONGWING TRAINING

Longwing training (and indeed flying) is generally a more complex proposition than shortwing training. I would advise taking a specialist longwing falconry course at a reputable centre, which will give you a solid foundation on which you can then build. The following will give you a flavour of what longwing training involves; if you are determined to fly falcons, then take it seriously and do it properly. It is very easy to practise falconry poorly.

At first, longwing training can progress rapidly, yet while they can appear relatively simple to train in the early stages, things really hot up when you near the flying stage. Bear this in mind!

Although you may not choose to hood your falcon immediately, it will need doing soon after you collect her so she gets used to it relatively early. Again, it is a bit of an art to surreptitiously slip a hood on, but it is something you will get the hang of with practice. At first, the falcon should be hooded for some time while she is carried around on the fist. You should both get used to taking off and putting on the hood, as well as tightening and loosening the braces (the leather straps built into the hood to pull it tight so it does not fall off).

Once the bird is happy with the hood, she can be persuaded, like a hawk, to feed off the fist. Again, this is not usually the trauma it is with shortwings,

but the same tactics apply; if she does not eat, then she gets no reward.

The next stage is stepping up, and can be carried out in much the same way as for shortwings. Some falconers believe that getting falcons to jump to the fist is a waste of time; others continue in the same way as they would for shortwings. In time, your falcon will probably jump up to meet you anyway because she is keen to fly, so training probably serves little purpose at this stage.

As mentioned earlier, introducing the swing lure is an important part of the falcon's early training to initiate her to its association with food. To begin, tie her rations to the lure and give the low whistle she will soon come to know so well as you swing the lure by your side. Then simply drop it in front of her and walk away. She will hop down for the food if she is hungry, and will have made the connection.

The next move is to get her to hop to the lure in the falconer's presence, when he can then practise 'making in' for the first time. This is the term used to describe the act of the falconer slowly approaching the bird after she has made a kill (or is eating on the lure). It should be done without upsetting the falcon too much, and when a suitably garnished fist is preferred to her she should swap over without realizing she has lost anything. This, as with all things in falconry, is not as easy as it looks.

When your falcon eventually deigns to jump down to the lure, you should make in slowly and quietly, keeping the lure line tight by running it through the lower fingers of the gloved hand while winding it onto the stick with the other.

Tip: always wind your lure line and indeed your creance in a figure of eight back onto the stick; normal round and round tying will simply end in a big knotted mess and will look untidy. The proper style will ensure your line can be fed out quickly and is held on safely.

If your falcon looks up and becomes agitated, you should stop and wait until she resumes feeding once more. When you are eventually close enough to ensure you can pick her up without unsettling her, she should be encouraged onto the glove. Once one step has been made, use the old trick of lifting your gloved hand to get her to step on with the other.

*You must be ready with your lure before you attempt to train your falcon; she will be coming at you
with breathtaking pace.*

Often, you will find she will bring the other foot up –
still clutching the lure or quarry (the same goes for
shortwings). Your only option is to manually
disentangle her, but beware while doing this,
particularly with shortwings!

Once the falcon is covering a decent distance on
the creance to the lure, this should be gradually
increased, remembering to give a low whistle and
swing the lure a couple of times before tossing it up
to one side and letting it fall to the ground. Also
remember to keep a foot on the creance, just in case
she flies past. It may be that she refuses to come as
the distance is increased, despite coaxing on your
behalf. Make sure you are not pushing her too far too
fast, and cut her back slightly. When she is coming
the length of the creance when you call, it is nearly
time for the maiden voyage.

Before this, however, it is sensible to assess
whether or not your bird intends to be a 'straight-

liner'. In other words, to determine whether your
bird will turn back to you after she has passed and
not received the lure, or whether she will continue
to fly on in a straight line, not knowing any better.
For her last flight on the creance, call her off and
hide the lure as soon as she is airborne. When she
has passed you, give a sharp blast on the whistle.
She should turn her head to look at you, expecting
to see the lure. When she does this, toss the lure out
for her, to the same side as she turned her head to
make things easy for her, and let her drop down for
it in the normal way. If she completes this
manoeuvre with little difficulty you can be
reasonably sure she will not disappear over the
horizon when you let her free. If she is still flying
onwards and needs to be brought to a halt by the
creance, then do not rush things; keep trying with
her until she realizes she must turn and come back
to you when the lure is not presented.

Longwings need to be very fit before they stand any chance of success in the field. Although they look magnificent on their blocks, they must be flown regularly.

So the momentous occasion has arrived. Place her on her fence post, walk away and give her a whistle, showing her the lure if necessary. When she is airborne, hide the lure and let her pass you, giving her a whistle as she climbs. There is no reason why she should not repeat the lesson she learned on the creance. Congratulations – now the really hard work starts!

For the first few lessons, simply let her get used to flying and gaining a little strength. Walk into wind with her, and after a few minutes during which she should circle you and explore the vicinity, bring her down to the lure. If she should show interest in disappearing or heading for a resting place at any time, whistle her up and toss down the lure. Do not overdo it at this stage, for if she gets tired she may well look for somewhere to rest, and once she has got into the habit you will be hard-pushed to stop her doing it. She will not gain a lot of height at this stage but do not fear, that will come with experience.

Longwings should not land in trees, so you do not want to get them used to the idea. Longwings are traditionally carried into the field with a hood covering their eyes so they cannot see. When quarry is spotted, the falcon is then unhooded and cast off to either chase or gain height ready for the quarry to be flushed by dog or falconer. If she catches it, she is picked up by the falconer; if she misses, she is called back by the use of the lure.

After a week or so of gradual fitness training, it is time to introduce your hawk to the lure to really get her to put some muscle on. Here is where your hours of solo training with the lure will pay off, for your lure-swinging needs to be top class now so as not to throw her out. At first, give her a couple of gradual passes so she gets the idea, but do not work her too hard. Build up the number of stoops as she gets fitter, and also increase the difficulty of the different types of pass until she is familiar with them. Always try and keep the lure just out of talon reach. You should get her used to catching the lure in the air at this point by giving a good blast on the whistle to let her know she can now have her prize, and tossing it up above your head as she comes in. Do not let go of the stick, for if you do you are likely to be left chasing the bird and lure for some distance. Instead, hang onto it and gently bring her back down to earth. If

she should ever catch you out and hit the lure, always let her have her reward, or she may feel cheated and start to tire of the whole procedure. A fit hawk should be able to make thirty or forty passes without undue strain. After two weeks of lure-swinging, you are ready to enter.

You may read elsewhere of the old practice of 'hacking back'. This is now almost non-existent, for it requires a wide area of secluded and suitable countryside. Basically, it involves creating a fake eyrie for an immature bird and allowing her to 'fledge' as she would in the wild, giving her several weeks of freedom before she is caught up again via a trap. In this way, she is a lot fitter than an aviary-bred bird and may even have learned a little of the etiquette of hunting. These birds can provide the falconer with the next best thing to a passager (wild-caught bird), although there are numerous problems associated with the practice, which once learned at hack are hard to overcome.

ETHICS

As I have continually stressed, falconry is about flying your trained bird at quarry in its wild habitat; nothing else will do, I'm afraid. If you find the idea of hunting live quarry distasteful, you should not take up falconry. By all means take on an owl if you can look after it properly, as it will no doubt give you a lot of pleasure. But that is not falconry. The sport is not for the squeamish. It is about wild things getting on with their natural urge to hunt and kill to eat.

However, in today's increasingly environmentally aware world, you will no doubt be tackled at some stage as to the validity of your actions.

For the record, I am an ex-shooter, against fox-hunting and hunting with hounds in general, but committed to keeping alive the viable, honourable and traditional ways of the British countryside. Those sentiments may seem at odds with each other, so I will try to explain.

Through the sport of shooting I gained most of my knowledge of the countryside and its intricate workings. I could not justify my sport for any of the usual reasons: because I owned a farm and pests and vermin were attacking my very livelihood; because I

You will inevitably be drawn into an argument on the ethics of the sport at some stage of your participation.

was short of food and so 'lived off the fat of the land'. The fact was my sport was just that: sport; killing for pleasure. While I am well aware that killing is but a small part of the true shooting enthusiast's love for his pastime, I nonetheless found that one day I could no longer tell myself that what I was doing was right. I remember the day perfectly.

It was late spring and the sun was warm. The trees were in blossom and wildlife was at its very best. I was out with my old shotgun (for the first time in many months) to escape for a few hours in peaceful solitude and contemplation. For me, that was one of the main reasons for going shooting. I could blend in with the surroundings, see some wonderful wildlife

up close, and relax and think without feeling the need to talk to anyone or behave in a certain fashion. It is true what hunters say: you *are* at one with nature.

Then, as I drowsed under a weeping willow and watched the natural world go about its business, I heard the unmistakable whisper of woodpigeon wings approaching from behind. (Anyone who knows the sound will tell you it cannot be mistaken for anything else; stock doves, collared doves and domestic pigeons have completely different flight sounds and movements.)

Instinctively, I looked up, saw the woodie float lazily over the hedge to my right not 20yd away, raised the gun and fired in a single, smooth movement. The crash of the shot was appallingly loud in the stillness of the afternoon and the pigeon crumpled in mid-air and planed to the ground with an audible thump some 30yd in front of me. My first feeling was one of surprise, for I had not pulled a trigger for months and had not expected to be able to hit a barn door at ten paces. Then, my heart sank as I saw the woodie, in a pile of white feathers, roll around, jump up and start to run, trailing one useless shattered wing. I gave chase and the contest was short and one-sided. Before I grabbed the bird up and dispatched it, for a split second we looked each other in the eyes. His were bright yellow and wide. His beak was flecked with blood and those beautiful plum-brushed breast feathers were ruffled in an obscene way. As I killed the bird I apologized to it and I have never shot at a living creature again. Soon afterwards I sold my guns.

I cannot really explain what was different about that woodie from the countless hundreds that I had cheerfully dispatched over the years, but I realized that what I was doing was fundamentally wrong.

I am not a rabid 'anti', indeed I still have the urge to grab a gun and get out there. I miss the whole stealth, skill and fieldcraft aspect, the glorious sunrises, the fiery sunsets, the after-dark lamping sessions for rabbits, the warm afterglow of that 'been hunting' feeling; but for me, at least, it is over. I believe that situation would instantly change, however, should I ever need to hunt for the pot again.

Being so close to nature for much of my life, I did not start to look at the countryside through rose-tinted glasses all of a sudden. I knew that 'red in tooth and claw' was a very apt phrase. None of my remorse and soul-searching is carried out (or needed) by predators and prey from the top to the

A bird's eye view; your raptor sees things in terms of predator and prey. There is no room for sentimentality in nature

bottom of the food chain. Do not be misled into looking at England's green and pleasant land and seeing fluffy bunnies and squawking birdies. Those same bunnies are slain by ferocious, many-toothed beasts and those birdies are hunted from the skies or ripped from the nests as babies by hungry predators.

So, what has all this to do with falconry? It has everything to do with falconry. When I discovered falconry, I was delighted that at last I had a reason to get back out into the countryside and once more become one with nature. What was more, I could do it with a clear conscience. Falconry is nothing more than allowing birds to do what they will do anyway; it simply involves us training them to tolerate our presence so we can have the privilege of watching them at work.

That is why I felt I could at last get involved in another 'country sport' that would give me the same thrills, sense of belonging and involvement in the countryside, without doing something my brain kept telling me was wrong. Falconry is the purest form of country sport, in my mind. It involves little

contrivance and is not killing for killing's sake. Some may argue with you on this point, saying that if you had not trained the hawk to kill, it would not have done so. By not training it to kill you are stifling one of its most powerful instincts, more immediate and powerful, I would suggest, than the desire to reproduce.

But why tether the bird to a perch so that it cannot fly, some will ask. Surely that is as cruel as putting a budgie in a tiny cage? No, again. In the wild, most predators do not while away their hours by gambling around the meadows or flitting from tree to tree. When they are sated they lounge around in the sun or perch on a favourite branch and have a doze. There is no unnecessary expense of energy. When the creature feels hungry enough to move, it does so and sets off hunting. So, when your hawk is on his bow or in his shelter, he is doing what he would be doing were he wild; just sitting and watching. When he is on flying weight, he is just hungry enough to hunt – and you take him out hunting. There is nothing cruel about that.

7 QUARRY – ITS HABITATS, HABITS AND HOW TO HUNT IT

LONGWING QUARRY

THE ROOK

The rook has long been regarded a worthy adversary for the falcon. These clever, gregarious birds nest in large rookeries and spend the day foraging together in the fields, searching out their favourite morsels such as leatherjackets and wireworms. They also take carrion, eggs and nestlings of other birds and can cause a lot of crop damage when they gather in sufficient numbers.

They are cunning, and as with their cousins, the raven and the jackdaw, they are superb fliers. Their aerobatics can be breathtaking as they attempt to avoid capture. The ideal rook flight is the classic 'ringing up' flight, when the prey

The silhouette of a rook.

climbs ever higher in an attempt to get above the hawk and avoid the deadly stoop. The falcon follows suit and these flights can end in a staggering earthward plummet at great speed.

Different types of falcon have been flown at rook with varying degrees of success, but, as always, most falconers turn to the ubiquitous peregrine, usually falcons (females) because of their greater bulk and power.

Grounded rooks can be vicious, and they have huge, dagger-like bills and sharp talons. Other members of the family often come to the aid of a captured colleague and there are records of falcons being blinded before the falconer could intervene.

Good rook country needs to be entirely devoid of cover, for these cunning birds will dive for the nearest available hideaway – there are even accounts of them seeking refuge under falconer's vehicles. The traditional rook hawker's Mecca was Salisbury Plain, where the falconers of the Old Hawking Club would gather each year for a couple of months of hard, fast sport over mile after mile of unspoilt land. These days, the Plain has been completely taken over by the military, and the vast open tracts of land are blotted by camps, firing ranges, fences and newly planted woods and copses, thus making them entirely unsuitable for the practice anymore.

Good 'slips' at rooks are quoted as essential for success. In other words, the odds must be stacked (or at least slightly pushed) in the hawk's favour. Therefore, the wind direction, location of nearest cover and topography of the land are vital factors when deciding whether or not the hawk is given a slip. Firstly, the hawk must be slipped into the wind with the feeding rooks directly upwind. As a general rule, cover should be twice the distance from the rooks than they are from the falcon before she is unhooded. Rooks find it hard making headway into the wind, whereas the falcon is far better suited to cutting through it. On many occasions, the hawk is slipped from a vehicle manoeuvred into the best possible position, but slips are also undertaken from the fist. I am reliably informed that regularly-hawked rooks recognize particular vehicles and take off as soon as they see them approach – so ensure you have a couple of cars handy! The hood should be removed and the hawk given time to compose herself and see the rooks. It is helpful at this point if the rooks flap a few yards, or more join their throng, for she will notice them all the quicker. Let her take off after them in her own time.

Passage rooks can also be tackled. These birds are best found on their regular flight lines from feeding ground to rookery, and need to be tested in open patches of land. Having the immediate advantage of height, these rooks are a trickier proposition and long flights, overhauling and capturing the quarry are more common than up-close, ringing flights.

If the rook makes it to cover and 'puts in', the decision has to be made whether or not to reflush it. It has to be calculated whether the hawk is able to 'wait-on' overhead while the quarry is reflushed, or whether she may get bored and set off self-hunting or even 'pitch' and settle herself down somewhere. When a kill is made, the falconer needs to get in quickly to avoid any damage to his bird.

The following is an account of spring rook hawking:

It was a very warm morning, and the rooks were feeding in a group of around six or so, more or less in the middle of a huge field about quarter of a mile from our position. We sat in the Land Rover on a gentle hill and so were several feet higher than the foraging rooks, who took no notice of us. There was little or no visible cover for them ahead, so we decided to slip a falcon at them.

She was slipped out of the window, and for around thirty seconds sat on the fist staring in the direction of the rooks. Then one of them flapped across a few yards to join his mates and she was away, slicing into the breeze and arrowing down the hillside towards them. I do not know whether they missed her outline against the backdrop of the coppiced hill, but it took some time before there was an almighty alarm squawk and the rooks exploded in all directions like splintered wood. By now, the peregrine was levelling out and gaining on them with deadly purpose. She zoomed up

behind one straggler and just as she seemed destined to pluck him from the sky, he dropped with a tumbling of his wings and turned to ride the wind back towards us. She overshot and lost valuable seconds.

As the frantic rook ploughed towards sanctuary the falcon seemed to change down a gear and allowed the wind to shoot her back towards the Land Rover. It was as if the rook was standing still. About 100yd from us and slightly downhill, she closed the gap and with surprising ease, stretched out a foot and simply grabbed him. Then she leisurely drifted down to the hillside and when we arrived, the panting falcon had him neatly trussed up, one foot wrapped around his head and the other pinioning both feet.

THE CROW

The silhouette of a crow.

Rook hawks are usually willing to tackle crows as well, which do not possess the powers of flight of the rook but are a more vicious prospect if captured. Crows spend most of their time alone or in pairs, feeding on a wide variety of foodstuffs including livestock feed and hens' eggs. Many farmers are only too pleased to be rid of them. They put into cover more readily than rooks and may have to be reflushed several times before they are caught. Make sure you get in quick if you intend to tackle this black-hearted villain, for his heavy bill is an imposing weapon.

THE MAGPIE
Continuing with the family corvidae, the magpie is about as cunning as they come, but is often hard to find in suitably open country for it rarely strays farther than sprinting distance from the nearest

cover. One falcon on its own – especially a youngster – would do well to successfully bag a magpie. In the past, a cast of falcons was utilized to capture this beautiful and elusive bird.

The magpie is adept at avoiding stoops, even though in many areas it may never actually have had to do it before. I have seen magpies avoid such attacks by falcons as if they had been doing it all their lives. But these birds lived in the south of England and were at the top of their food chain. Nothing

The silhouette of a magpie.

other than man ever killed them. They could not have been attacked from the sky for generations. I suppose it is possible that a wild sparrowhawk may have attempted to take one, but sparrowhawks very rarely stoop anyway and the presumption that a wild spar would take on a magpie when it could nab a nearby finch is pretty preposterous. (Trained sparrowhawks can and do take magpies and a cast is deemed ideal for the job.) Hard-pressed magpies will ensconce themselves in the meagrest of cover to avoid a falcon overhead and are difficult to dislodge once put in. As witnessed by Philip Glasier, they will even dive into a flock of sheep for cover, and cling onto one of its members to pass unnoticed. It seems there is some instinctive behaviour in wildlife that is simply passed on, whether regularly used or not.

Magpies are notorious thieves and have a terrible reputation for stealing eggs and nestlings of songbirds. Although this has undoubtedly been wildly exaggerated over the years, they do account for a significant number of thefts, simply because their prying eyes do not miss a trick in their neighbourhood; the comings and goings of a nesting

pair of blackbirds, for example, is simply too obvious for a magpie to miss.

Much of the magpie's diet is made up of small vertebrates, such as insects, lizards and the occasional vole. They will pluck butterflies out of the air as a tasty apéritif and have a taste for carrion. I once saw a magpie leaping and hopping animatedly in the middle of a field, stabbing repeatedly into the ground with its bill. Upon investigation, I found the bird had been wrestling with a mole. The bloodied creature eventually, under my guardianship, escaped by digging safely underground.

The European magpie that we see in the UK is similar in many ways to the yellow-billed variety found in many parts of the States. They are both precocious and intelligent and both horde large amounts of food for hard times. Studies have revealed these larders can number thousands, and the magpie seems to remember the exact location of most of them.

Like the rest of its kin, the magpie is going from strength to strength because of its adaptive nature and also because, in much of its range, it has no predators. Only the goshawk ever takes this bird with any degree of regularity. In winter the magpie can gather in large numbers and 'treetop' (spending time calling and displaying in the very tops of trees and hedgerows).

THE GULL

The smaller common and black-headed gulls are protected in the UK and the falconer will need a licence from the Department of the Environment to take them.

The larger gulls apparently lack the mobility of the smaller species and are therefore taken more easily by the falcon. Gull hawking can be a rewarding pastime, for the only cover gulls will use is water; they will not put in elsewhere. Chases can therefore be long and arduous and the falconer should be ready with his telemetry in enclosed country.

More and more in the south of England, gulls can be found inland, indeed there are those that I am sure have never seen the sea let alone been on a lonely, storm-tossed journey across one. They congregate behind ploughing farmers and in great numbers at rubbish tips. Unfortunately, here they are joined by a host of other scavengers and a falcon would easily be convinced into taking another species.

THE PHEASANT

The silhouette of a pheasant.

Generally regarded as the poor man's version of grouse, pheasant hawking is not easily undertaken by the longwing fan because, by their very nature, pheasants spend a large amount of their time in or near woodland and therefore in the wrong kind of territory for falcons. Pheasants are best left to the shortwings to tackle.

THE DUCK

This kind of longwing flying can result in some spectacular chases, but needs dedication and practice on the part of both falconer and bird to succeed.

The silhouette of a duck.

Tip: we are talking about wild duck here, rather than the tame, fat, quacking specimens you find on the village pond. These could be caught by the least vicious poodle and so have no place in the falconer's game book. It is wild duck we are after, and a truly sporting proposition they are.

Duck hawking can involve a lot of activity on the falconer's behalf, for when pressed, the duck will head back to water; indeed they may need persuasion to leave it at all if they notice the falcon waiting on overhead. It is best to get the help of an experienced duck hawker if at all possible, otherwise the wild duck will easily get the better of you. The location and topography of the area surrounding the duck pond is also crucial to successful flights, and an experienced duck hawker will be able to tell you which ones are worth a slip and which are best left alone.

THE PARTRIDGE

The methods of partridge hawking are similar in many respects to those of the famous grouse hawking (see below), but are carried out on much lower ground because that is where partridges are to be found. Many falconers have also had some good sport of their own making by putting down partridges on their hawking territory. Although this is an excellent proposition for those with both the time and the money, captive partridges are never as quick and wily as their wild counterparts (at least not until later in the season).

Renowned for taking advantage of the flimsiest of cover available to them, partridges are no mean quarry and will put on a good show. But the terrain must be devoid of as much cover as possible, and because of the very nature of the contour-hugging, quick exploding flights, barbed wire fences and similar can be lethal to your hawk.

A friend told me of an acquaintance who was unfortunately one of those falconers who would not listen to reason, and so bought himself a falcon even though he lived in the south of England in extremely enclosed countryside. He trained it, went to all the expense of buying equipment, fancy mews, even partridge poults for the couple of nearby fields he had permission to hawk over. Three weeks into his flying season, his falcon was closing fast when the cunning partridge put in just beneath a wire fence. The tiercel's head was taken clean off his shoulders.

THE GROUSE

This is what longwing flying is really all about. Grouse are considered the ultimate sporting quarry among shooters, and are held in similar regard by falconers. This is a rigorous art form, seriously hard to undertake and twice as hard to achieve competence in. There are not many who would truthfully claim to have mastered it. You need to dedicate many months of the year to grouse hawking; you need access to exclusive grouse moors for considerable lengths of time; you need suitable accommodation in which to put up your birds, dogs and various hawking party guests; you need a lot of money, it seems, these days. Only a few falconers are privileged enough to see this kind of hawking these days; fewer still actually get to practise it.

The silhouette of a partridge.

The basics seem simple enough. The hawking party heads up to the traditional grouse moors with a party of falcons (peregrines have proven they are by far the best for this sort of sport, particularly the females). The falconers, with their dogs and birds, head out onto the moor, and when the dog picks up the scent of a covey (group of grouse) it goes on point, giving the falconer a good idea of where the birds are lying up, hoping to avoid detection.

Now the falconer has plenty of time, because the grouse will not move until flushed. The falcon is unhooded and allowed to take her own time to look around, rouse and then set off to climb into the sky. The experienced hawk will climb very high indeed and circle over the falconer and dog, watching for the expected help from below. Just as she reaches the correct position and is looking down, the falconer gives his whistle and the dog goes in. The covey gets up, the falcon stoops and hopefully knocks a bird out of the sky.

It is a breathtaking privilege to witness such an incredible display of speed, power and timing at close quarters. Most of us can only dream of it. Below is an account of a morning's grouse hawking, courtesy of a falconer who received the trip to Scotland as a 30th birthday present.

It was much wetter and windier than I had been expecting and it was damned cold too! The moors looked pretty desolate and, I have to admit, the thought of clambering out of the warm Land Rover as we neared our destination was not particularly appealing. In the back was a box cadge, and sitting on it four immaculate peregrines. They wore splendid hoods and sat quietly, only the occasional jingling of a leg bell making them cock their covered heads to listen. Also in the back, curled and apparently unconcerned, were a couple of German short-haired pointers.

Eventually disembarkation was necessary, and we stepped out into a high wind, speckled with icy arrows of rain. It was not pleasant, but after much ado the party set off, heading upwards to higher ground.

After about half an hour of making our way across the heather, one of the dogs, which had been quartering beautifully all along, stopped and went on point. The falconer called in his other dog and gathered the party up, positioning us for the best vantage point away to the right and slightly higher than the dog and invisible covey. The falcon was removed from the field cadge and unhooded, the falconer's fist held high as she took stock of her surroundings, eyed the dog and then roused hard. Then she leapt purposefully from the glove after a couple of minutes, and ploughed into the wind, cutting through it with seeming ease and quickly gaining height, all the while turning her head this way and that to watch the falconer below. She climbed steadily until she reached quite a height, several hundred feet I would say, and then glided in large circles above us. Just as she reached a turn and was looking over her shoulder to keep an eye on the action, the falconer sent the dog in. The covey exploded from right under her nose and simultaneously the falcon tipped a wing and dropped like a drip from a tap.

She came in at an angle, incredibly fast but also incredibly controlled, as though she was on some invisible line or wire in the sky. I could not hazard a guess at her speed when she reached the covey, but it must have been prodigious, for when she struck one of the stragglers as she whipped above it, the noise was startlingly loud. A cloud of feathers burst from the unfortunate grouse and it fairly crashed to the ground, bouncing several feet in the air before coming to a stop among the heather, perfectly dead already from the force of the attack. The ferocity and deadly perfection of the attack brought an exclamation from the lips of every member of the party.

The falcon swept back up into the air after the attack and almost performed a loop-the-loop, coming back down to grab the grouse on the ground. Mantling over the game bird she looked about her warily and quickly began tearing out great tufts of feathers to get at the warm flesh within.

To reach this stage of success takes an incredible amount of time. Just imagine; we have spent the whole of this book discussing the various methods of hawking and training. Now combine those with training a dog as well. It is enough to send a shiver down your spine!

A gundog simply will not do. The last thing you need when attempting the tricky business of flying your longwing is to have to chase halfway across the moor for your errant dog. The dog (traditionally a setter or pointer) needs to be able to respond to hand signals and whistles (not forgetting that these whistles must be distinct from the ones for your hawk) and must be able to remain steady on point for several minutes at a time. The dog also needs to be taught to point only grouse; it will find itself with a very angry falconer indeed if it eventually flushes a hare while the falcon waits on overhead. Apparently pointers do not reach their best for several seasons, so a veteran mixed with a youngster is often called for. As you can see, things get more and more complicated. Add to this the factors that can upset the best laid plans: weather, dog wandering off, hawk wandering off, wild birds of prey mobbing your bird or scaring off the grouse, and unsuitable terrain.

It was always my aim to make grouse hawking sound daunting, as it is. This should go some way to putting off those falconers who believe they could 'give it a try' simply because it is arguably the

ultimate falconing test. Do not be tempted into it unless you have lots of money, dedication, determination, a love of the sport and wildlife and plenty of time on your hands. If, like me, you are determined to experience it first hand at some stage, start saving your pennies. At the time of writing, there is the possibility that I may fulfil this dream; if it happens, it will make a book in itself!

SHORTWING QUARRY

THE RABBIT
This species will form the staple part of any shortwing hunting. The rabbit is well-known to us all, whether we live in the city or countryside, for the adaptable coney can be found almost anywhere there is a patch of scrub grass and somewhere for its burrow.

The silhouette of a rabbit.

Despite massive culls across the country, numbers are so large that rabbits are the most commonly seen wild mammal in the country. Man very nearly did achieve its eradication, however, when he introduced the terrible myxomatosis, or 'myxy' as country dwellers call it. This highly infectious disease spread from rabbit to rabbit via fleas, therefore when one infected rabbit came back to the warren, it effectively sealed the doom of its cousins. Affecting the eyes in a hideous way, the disease blinded the rabbits and left them shuffling helplessly around, unable to see any oncoming predator and effectively waiting to die.

The resilient rabbits have developed some form of immunity to it these days, although it does return in bouts, and cleans the rabbits out of an area every now and then.

Large numbers of rabbits can be incredibly destructive, not only to crops. Their rapid breeding rate means they are constantly expanding and digging more burrows (incidentally, the does do virtually all the digging). This in turn causes huge erosion and destruction of the natural habitat. If allowed to breed unchecked, rabbits can reduce a particular area to a virtual wilderness.

Although dawn and dusk are optimum times for catching rabbits out feeding, there are usually one or two to be caught 'up top' most times of the day. They particularly dislike high winds and heavy rain.

Hawking rabbits can be done in one of several ways. Simply by wandering along hedgerows quietly with your hawk following on can yield good results; your hawk will more often than not spot them before you and go crashing into the undergrowth, but sometimes it is surprising how the birds can miss one that is seemingly under their nose. In these circumstances, a little help from the falconer usually does the trick. Some exciting, if brief, chases and captures can follow with this relaxed and 'rough hawking' style of sport.

Alternatively, rabbit hawking can be undertaken from the fist in a similar 'walked up' fashion. Here, it is best not to grab hold of your bird's jesses as you travel, for when she suddenly seems to leap from your fist for no apparent reason, you will be tempted to restrain her. Again, more often than not she will have seen quarry long before you and your restraint will cost her a decent slip. It is preferable, if at all possible, not to restrain your hawk while out in the field.

If rabbits are proving hard to track down above ground, they can be successfully ferreted out for the hawks to chase. Obviously, care has to be taken to ensure the hawk and ferret are amenable work colleagues, otherwise the end game is likely to result in a win for the hawk.

Tip: use a white ferret, as this is less likely to be associated with food – and then remember not to feed your bird white rats.

Some advocate lamping rabbits with hawks, but I do not hold with this. The idea is that one person holds a lamp trained on a rabbit (as in shooting – the rabbits will be mesmerized by the glare), while another sets the hawk off after it. If the rabbit moves, the lamper should follow it with the beam (what happens if there is a fence, or trees, or the light is blocked suddenly?). Then, supposedly, the hawk either catches or misses and should be brought back to the glove by shining the light on it when well-garnished. This seems too risky to me. What happens if the hawk crashes into an unseen object in the dark? What happens if, because of obstructions from cover, he cannot see your glove and you cannot see him? Take my advice and stick to daylight rabbit hawking; this is hard enough without turning the lights out.

THE HARE (BLUE AND BROWN)

Of the two hare species, the larger brown is probably most common because its habitat is more open, flat grassland. The blue hare, which changes to a snow white in its northern range, is a creature of the mountains and moors.

The silhouette of a hare.

Hares are a big proposition for any hawk, with an impressive turn of speed and a powerful kick. That is why, for the most part, they are taken by the bigger hawks, female harrises, redtails, and so on. Hares are usually walked up, like rabbits, but can also be flown with the shortwing slope-soaring. By its very nature, this requires some hilly country where the bird can get uplift from the slope and differing air pressures and temperatures. In this way, they can perform their own kind of waiting on, and have the advantage of height when hares are flushed and begin to run.

Typically, hares set off at a decent lope to start with, but when they realize things are dangerous, really let rip and seem to fly across the ground at great speed. They also leap and jink to avoid capture, and hare flights, because of their generally open nature, are easily seen and can last a relatively long time. Particularly when flying a cast or more of harrises, males will be tempted to take a hare on because they know they have back up on the way. Most hare flights do end in failure because of the bucking strength of the mammal. A firm head grip is needed, and the falconer should make in as quickly as possible to help, because the powerful kick of the hare is reputed to be enough to cause serious injury to a struggling shortwing.

Hares are distinguished from the rabbit by their far greater size, their huge hind legs and the dark tips to their long ears.

THE SQUIRREL

The grey squirrel is the most common species of squirrel these days, and the only one listed as a quarry species as the red is protected.

Firstly, squirrels should be avoided if at all possible. It is always with reluctance that I say this, for squirrel hawking is excellent sport and very exciting to watch. But that excitement is always marred by anxiety, for the grey is capable of causing very nasty bite injuries to your hawk if it is not trussed up sufficiently by her feet. I have heard stories of petty singles being bitten clean off by caught squirrels, and nasty lacerations of the feet are commonplace. There is little you can do if your hawk is determined to catch a squirrel; you should simply try and avoid them in the first place as far as possible. They are woodland creatures on the whole, so avoid the obvious places. They are, on occasion, caught completely out in the open, a long way from trees, and have been known to make their dreys in old rabbit burrows in particularly treeless areas. If

your hawk does capture a squirrel, move in quick to dispatch it.

Incidentally, contrary to popular belief, grey squirrels do not hibernate, but merely lay up in their dreys on the worst days. In the depths of winter they will forage for sustenance on bright sunny days.

THE PHEASANT

Shortwings can excel at pheasant, and wild birds provide excellent sport. Young birds tend to be a little easy, but the wily old cocks and hens are much more of a test and will quickly outfly most hawks unless caught on the ground.

Most flights start when the pheasant is spotted on the ground, and may continue into flight as the game bird is hard-pressed. But immature birds are regularly outfoxed by pheasants. The pheasant waits until the last second, when the hawk is preparing to crash in onto it, then leaps into the air in an explosive take-off with that unforgettable whirr of wings. More often than not, the hawk will be left stranded as the pheasant makes good its escape. Sometimes, the hawk may get a footfull of feathers, as Archie did on repeated occasions in his first season. It takes some time for hawks to get the knack of binding on properly, and it also takes a more experienced bird to realize that all may not be lost once the pheasant has evaded the first attack. Pheasants seldom fly far, and will put in again a little further away. The veteran pheasant hawk will continue the chase and attempt to take them again and again, or will mark the spot and wait for assistance from the falconer.

Pheasants are found in and around woodland (beware of squirrels) and are a splendid addition to the falconer's pot. The birds also have a taste for them, so it may be fair to let your hawk have a treat every now and then as a reward for her efforts!

THE DUCK

The same rules apply as for hunting ducks with longwings. Wild ducks are the ones you should be after, and again, they are a very tricky proposition for all but the best of hawks.

Once in full flight, hawks have no chance of getting within grabbing distance of ducks, so the falconer must engineer the slip so that the bird can be taken on the ground or during attempted take-off.

Not many ducks are successfully taken on water; the bird just dives the moment the hawk plunges in and you are left with a wet and sorry-looking hawk.

Most successful duck hawks take their quarry on dry land, and the falconer needs to help his bird by getting her close by without the duck noticing. Getting her positioned in a tall tree is a good move and allows her to make her own mind up on a strategy. If there are islands on your duck pond be prepared to take a dip!

THE PARTRIDGE

A quick and agile bird and one which every shortwing man (or austringer) is very pleased to see on his territory. The two main varieties in the UK are the red-legged and the grey, mostly bred for shooting.

Greys are slightly smaller and are the most common. Partridges are normally found by walked up hawking, although this is difficult in some of their patches where they stick to the middle of large fields and therefore have an excellent view of any oncoming predators. Careful observation is advisable to see where the partridge coveys lie up and where they can best be approached with judicious use of available cover. Even so, the falconer will be very pleased to have the name 'partridge' entered into his game book, for once on the wing these little birds fly like the wind.

The fortunate falconer with his own hunting territory (or an amenable landowner) could consider putting down some birds of his own in small shelters spaced out over his shoot. Gradually, the birds are allowed to wander, still using the shelters as a base, and then become fully wild after a good start in life. It is better to get your hawk used to them relatively early before they become truly wild when they will prove far too elusive for anything but the fittest and most competent hawks.

THE MOORHEN

Moorhen are quite regularly taken by hawks, as is their cousin, the coot. Although some consider them too easy for a good hawk, they are excellent practice for a youngster and by no means a pushover. Coots in particular can put on a fair lick of speed when they need to.

These water birds are mostly found around duck ponds and drainage ditches, and much to the annoyance of the duck hawker, the bird sensibly chooses the coot or moorhen as the more catchable option. Both have a habit of diving underwater just as the hawk stoops and has to throw up into an overhanging tree to await the reflush. This style of water hawking can be great fun as the coots and moorhens dive for cover and the bird hunts them down along the water's edge. On occasion, this does, however, result in an escaped coot and a soggy bird of prey.

One must be careful not to overdo this style of rough hawking with young hawks. They may become so particular to the water birds that they refuse to tackle quicker, more elusive prey.

VARIOUS

The various section in your game book will probably stack up just as many kills as the 'proper' quarry species.

The silhouette of a pigeon. The 'various' category of your game book will feature a number of species, including the woodpigeon. Do not let your birds eat pigeon though; they commonly have a disease known to falconers as frounce, which affects the mouth and throat.

Among those species regularly taken by hawks are weasels and stoats (which both stink to high heaven and will taint your hawking glove for days); rats; the occasional corvid such as a crow or magpie, although generally they are too clever to come near; small mammals such as mice and voles; small birds can sometimes be snatched out of the air; indeed one day, much to my shame in front of a gathered party of friends and relatives, Archie stooped nicely from an overhead tree and caught a small frog. Of course, he ate it with much relish.

I always try to avoid taking songbirds, and in fact most of the bigger species seem to ignore them. Harrises have an unfortunate fascination with little owls, and although flights at them are spectacular, one hates to catch these charming creatures. Again, though, there is little one can do when a bird spots something and decides to go for it. On occasion it is possible to get to the caught quarry before too much damage is done and release it surreptitiously to fight another day while your bird feeds up on a tasty morsel.

Incidentally, on one of my hunting territories one little owl regularly flaunted himself at us until chased. He always managed to get away in time and dive into a hole in an oak tree. I just hope he does not lose his timing as he gets older!

When your bird catches, make in quickly if it needs help. It does no good to our sport to see captured animals suffer unnecessarily. Let your bird have a small reward if she is to carry on for another couple of slips, but if she is young, then let her have her fill and do not rob her. Do not ask her to do too much too soon.

When hunting, it is best to steer clear of all other people. At best, they will pester you with questions and ruin the peace and quiet of your hawking. At worst they may take offence at you being there or scare your hawk off with their dog or horse. I always live in fear that an old lady with one of those tiny rat-like dogs will appear out of nowhere in front of my hungry hawk. Now that would take some explaining…

EPILOGUE

I hope you have found something of use to you in this book, whether to satisfy curiosity, whet the appetite or provide a useful guide.

If you are still considering taking up the sport, devour all the literature you can find. Most falconers still spend small fortunes on falconry books and are always eager to read more. Book yourself a couple of days at a reputable falconry centre and learn the basics. As in most things, there is no substitute for a knowledgeable and patient tutor.

If you have determined that the sport is not for you, then I doff my cap to you. You have acted in a responsible manner and have not damaged either the sport's reputation or the health of a hawk by taking

Do not attempt to keep a bird unless you can afford the time; a goshawk, for instance, requires handling and flying every day if possible.

Look after your bird and your equipment. Grease your leather jesses regularly...

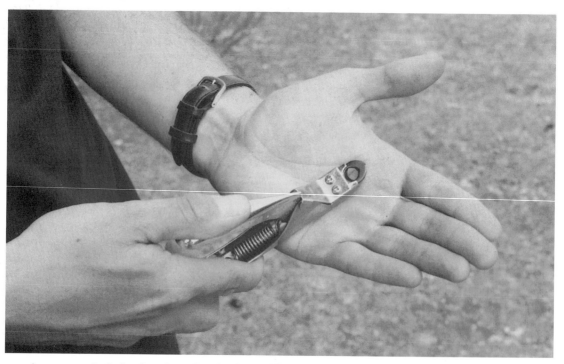

...and carry out routine husbandry such as talon-trimming carefully and with suitable instruments, like these clippers.

With enough effort and some good fortune, you will build a fabulous rapport with your bird. Make the most of it.

on a bird when you cannot do it justice. Perhaps your circumstances will change and you will be able to follow the sport in the future.

Whatever your reasons and choices, I hope *On a Wing and a Prayer* will lead you on to further exploits and pleasures associated with this most magnificent of traditions.

For what could be better on a cold and dank winter's day than a few hours spent in the companionship of your working bird? When clouds hang low and biting winds cut across the countryside, whipping crows across the skyline like charred pieces of paper; when sleet is angled into shards that slice into your face until it surrenders to numbness; when the trees shudder, skeletal and desolate, as winter closes its icy fist on the world; when all living things think of nothing more than survival for one more interminable day; then you will be joyous among them. For you will be free from the worries of life for those few hours.

Free from the restraints of cars and jobs and people and money. Free, like the very bird that pitches and soars above you.

EXTRACTS FROM MY TRAINING DIARY (SEASON 1998–99)

Thursday 24 September: I first saw Archie tonight, already jessed up and sitting on the lawn at The English School of Falconry. By Murphy's Law, I am due to go on holiday this weekend, so the first stages of his manning will have to wait a week. Typical.

Saturday 3 October: Picked Archie up at last and brought him home. It was obvious he had learned little from the other, more civilized harrises who sat with him on the weathering lawn. He is hissing, spitting, wild. Settled him into his night quarters and let him be.

Sunday 4 October: Long manning walk ... I was pleased to see him spending more and more time on the fist ... Archie discovered his bath for the first time ... could not be persuaded to feed from the fist,

hope he will tomorrow. It will be the start of his third day without food.

Monday 5 October: YES! Finally persuaded him to eat (not without a little trickery) at 5pm ... finished the day nicely with him stepping back onto his perch ... feel like I am making progress.

Tuesday 6 October: Lesson has been learned; fed from fist immediately ... got him on scales to check in at 1lb 6oz ... has discovered the benefits of a bath and his tail is benefiting as a result.

Wednesday 7 October: Persuaded him to step up for food without too many problems, although he has a touch of 'sticky foot', which is to be expected ... the speed at which he learns is pretty impressive.

Learn what you can about different species; each has its own quirks and characteristics.

With careful management, your bird should give you years of pleasure.

The end of a snowy hawking afternoon.

Thursday 8 October: Jumped to the fist without too much trouble.

Friday 9 October: Only the opportunity for a brief evening flight due to work commitments, but he came 6ft!

Saturday 10 October: Transported him successfully in the car to my parents' house, where he enjoyed a bath and the afternoon blocked out in the sun.

Sunday 11 October: Needs cutting back … is coming 20yd or so on the creance already, but only in his own sweet time … he will have to learn the hard way.

Monday 12 October: Slightly lower weight; performance much better.

For the rest of this week, strong winds severely hamper training. On Wednesday, though, he came the length of the creance. When winds die, it is with a hammering heart that I decide to undergo the maiden voyage.

Thursday 15 October: He was sitting on the lowest branch of a horse chestnut tree – completely untethered. I forced myself to walk 30yd or so and turned, heart in throat, to whistle. He came! Straight to the glove, without hesitation. To say I am delighted is an understatement.

The following days moved into weeks as we followed on, then practised with the dummy bunny. A couple of chases followed, then the fateful excursion recounted earlier made Archie an entered bird and me a falconer proper. May our game book be long and forever eventful.

GLOSSARY

This is not an exhaustive list of falconry terms, but it is a good starting point. The language of the sport is rich, colourful, and sometimes confusing, but you will notice some familiar terms which are used in everyday language; these have been 'soaked up' from the time when falconry was known to much of the general public.

Accipiter   Shortwinged hawk with rounded wings and yellow eyes.

Austringer   Someone who flies hawks rather than falcons.

Aylmeri   Leather anklets through which jesses are fed.

Bate   To fly from the fist or perch; sometimes in fear, sometimes in eagerness/anticipation of flying.

Bells   Bells are fitted to the hawk to enable the falconer to hear her on quarry or in cover. Traditionally made of brass.

Bewit   Leather strap used to attach the bells to the hawk's legs.

Bind   To grab and hold onto.

Block   Outdoor perch favoured for falcons.

Bloom   The natural waterproofing on the feathers.

Bow perch   Outdoor perch favoured for hawks.

Break in   To break through the skin of the prey to start eating.

Bowse   To drink. The term 'boozing', referring to drinking alcohol, has derived from 'bowse'.

Bumblefoot   An infection of the foot that is very difficult to remove. It shows itself via reddening, swelling, heat, or black dots and scaly, hard patches under the foot.

Cadge   A perch devised to carry several falcons at once. The traditional cadge is a wooden frame, upon which the falcons sit hooded and tethered. It is fitted with straps that go over the cadger's shoulders when he is in the centre of the frame, thus allowing him to wander about and carry the birds quite safely. A box cadge is exactly what it says: a box used to transport birds in a similar fashion in the car.

Cadger   The person (traditionally a young boy) who carries the cadge. The term 'cadger' as we know it is believed to come from the fact that the boy would tell on-lookers a little about his birds – including some very tall tales – to ply them for money.

Cast   Falconry's most oversubscribed word! A cast of hawks is two hawks; to cast a hawk is to set it off from the fist; it is also to safely hold the bird so it can be fitted with furniture; a hawk also casts by throwing up a pellet of indigestible bone, feather and fur from its last meal.

Castings   The pellet of undigested bone, fur and feather from the last meal.

Cere   The waxy area above the beak.

Condition   The flying state of the hawk; if in low condition the hawk is thin and undernourished, when high it is too fat.

Cope   To shorten, file and shape the beak and talons.

Crab   Hawks grabbing hold of each other are said to 'crab'.

Creance   The thin line attached to the bird prior to its first free flight.

Crop   The pouch in which food is first stored in hawks and falcons before it is passed to the stomach.

Deck feathers   The two centre feathers of the tail.

Enter   To successfully kill for the first time.

Eyass   A bird taken from an eyrie (now used to describe all young falcons).

Eyrie   A falcon or eagle nesting site.

Falcon   The female peregrine, now also used to refer to females of other falcon species.

Feak The action of stropping the beak clean after eating.

Fed up A bird who has eaten her daily rations.

Flight feathers The primaries, secondaries and tail feathers: the main feathers used in flight.

Foot The action of striking with the feet.

Gleam The substance coating the casting.

Gorge To allow the hawk to feed as much as she wants.

Hack An old-fashioned method of rearing young hawks to keep them flying free.

Hack back To gradually release an unwanted bird back to the wild.

Haggard A female falcon caught in mature plumage.

Hard down When all the new feathers are completely grown and bloodless.

Hawk Strictly an accipiter, but used generally as a term to cover both hawks and falcons.

Hood The leather cap placed over a falcon's (or hawk's) head to cover its vision.

Hybrid Cross-breed.

Imp The process of replacing broken or damaged flight feathers.

Imprinting Behaviour occurring when the bird is not properly parent-reared.

Jesses Leather straps around a hawk's legs used to hold on to a bird or help attach it to a perch.

Keen A hawk responding quickly and looking eager is said to be 'keen'.

Leash Usually a short length of Terylene rope, used to actually tether the bird down to a perch.

Longwing Used to describe all falconidae.

Lure A simulation bird or animal used to train the bird to hunt, get it fit and bring it back to the falconer.

Make in To approach the bird on the ground to pick it up, usually after a kill.

Man To tame a hawk, making it used to man and his surroundings.

Mantle The action of a hawk on food; the wings are spread out over the food to try and hide it from other predators.

Mark down To pinpoint the place in which a hawk or its quarry has gone to cover.

Mews The place where hawks are traditionally kept and moulted.

Mutes Hawk excrement.

Passage hawk An immature hawk caught during migration.

Pitch To land on a perch (particularly falcons); and the height at which a falcon begins her stoop.

Petty singles A hawk's toes.

Pick-up piece Piece of meat used to entice the bird during training or in the field.

Pounces Talons.

Primaries The main wing feathers.

Put in When quarry dives into cover.

Put out When quarry dives out of cover.

Put over When the crop is emptied into the stomach.

Quarry The game hawked at.

Rake away To fly off to one side.

Ring up To fly upwards in circles.

Rouse To ruffle the plumage into position in a convulsive shake.

Sails The wings of a hawk.

Soaring When a hawk flies high and easily, seemingly enjoying just flying and not hunting.

Spar Shorter term for a sparrowhawk.

Stoop To descend rapidly from a height with folded wings.

Stropping Otherwise known as feaking; the action of wiping the beak clean after eating on a handy perch or rock.

Swivel The metal piece of equipment attached to both jesses and leash to prevent them tangling.

Tiring A tough piece of meat given to a hawk during manning to occupy her.

Tiercel A male peregrine, now also used to describe the males of other species.

Wait on The action of a hawk flying overhead, waiting for game to be flushed.

Weather The action of putting your bird outside on its perch.

Weathering The place where birds are weathered.

Yarak A delicious Eastern word; a fit hawk in fine flying condition is said to be 'in Yarak'.

The redtail is a beautiful hawk, and in maturity does indeed grow rufous-coloured tail feathers.

USEFUL ADDRESSES

The English School of Falconry
Bedford Road
Husborne Crawley
Bedfordshire
MK43 0UT
Tel: 01908 281229

The British School of Falconry at Gleneagles
The Gleneagles Hotel
Perthshire
Scotland
PH3 1NF
Tel: 01764 62231

The Hawk Conservancy
Weyhill
Nr Andover
Hampshire
SP11 8DY
Tel: 01264 772252

The National Birds of Prey Centre
Newent
Gloucestershire
GL18 1JG
Tel: 01531 820286

Falconry Originals (equipment)
3 Haughton Mill Cottages
Haughton
Nr Retford
Nottinghamshire
DN22 8DY
Tel: 01623 836071

Martin Jones (equipment)
The Lodge
Huntley
Gloucestershire
GL19 3HG
Tel: 01452 830629

The British Falconer's Club
c/o John Fairclough
Home Farm
Hints
Nr Tamworth
Staffordshire
B78 3DW
Tel: 01543 481737

Neil Forbes
(specialist bird-of-prey veterinary)
Lansdown Veterinary Group
The Clockhouse Veterinary Hospital
Wallbridge Road
Stroud
Gloucestershire
GL5 3JD
Tel: 01453 672555

BIBLIOGRAPHY

Baker, J. A. *The Peregrine*
(Collins, 1967)

Ford, E. *Falconry Art and Practice*
(Blandford 1992)

Glasier, P. *Falconry and Hawking*
(B.T. Batsford Ltd, 1978)

Glasier, P. *As The Falcon Her Bells*
(Heinemann, 1963)

Hammond, N. and Pearson, B. *Birds of Prey*
(Hamlyn, 1993)

Upton, R. *Falconry, Principles and Practice*
(A & C Black, 1991)

Woodford, M. H. *A Manual of Falconry*
(A & C Black, 1960)

The author with Archie.

The tawny eagle is a big, powerful bird and a notorious pirate.

INDEX